This Was Not America

A Wrangle Through
Jewish-Polish-American History

Cherry
Orchard
Books

This Was Not America

A Wrangle Through
Jewish-Polish-American History

Elżbieta Janicka
Michael Steinlauf

BOSTON
2022

Library of Congress Cataloging-in-Publication Data

Names: Janicka, Elżbieta, author, interviewer. | Steinlauf, Michael C., interviewee, translator.
Title: This was not America : a wrangle through Jewish-Polish-American history / Elżbieta Janicka, Michael Steinlauf.
Description: Boston : Cherry Orchard Books, 2022. | "This book began in 2014 when Elżbieta Janicka approached Michael Steinlauf about the possibility of conducting a long, multifaceted interview with him. Such an endeavor is a Polish genre known as wywiad-rzeka, interview-river. Over the following years, Janicka and Steinlauf met in Warsaw and Philadelphia, recorded their conversations, in Polish, and assembled them into a narrative which was published in a journal of the Institute of Slavic Studies of the Polish Academy of Sciences. An expanded version was translated by Steinlauf into English. In your hands or on your screen, dear reader, are the results."--Preface. | Includes bibliographical references.
Identifiers: LCCN 2022003032 (print) | LCCN 2022003033 (ebook) | ISBN 9781644698396 (hardback) | ISBN 9781644698402 (paperback) | ISBN 9781644698419 (adobe pdf) | ISBN 9781644698426 (epub)
Subjects: LCSH: Steinlauf, Michael C. | Steinlauf, Michael C.--Family. | Polish Americans--Interviews. | Jews--United States--Interviews. | Children of Holocaust survivors--United States--Interviews. | Holocaust survivors--Poland. | Holocaust survivors--United States. | Jewish refugees--United States--Interviews.
Classification: LCC DS134.56 .J36 2022 (print) | LCC DS134.56 (ebook) | DDC 305.892/40438--dc23/eng/20220121
LC record available at https://lccn.loc.gov/2022003032
LC ebook record available at https://lccn.loc.gov/2022003033

ISBN 9781644698396 (hardback)
ISBN 9781644698402 (paperback)
ISBN 9781644698419 (adobe pdf)
ISBN 9781644698426 (epub)

Cover design by Ivan Grave.
On the cover: The Steinlauf family, c. 1954. For details, please see p. 51
Book design by Lapiz Digital Services.

Published by Cherry Orchard Books, an imprint of Academic Studies Press
1577 Beacon Street
Brookline, MA, 02446, USA
press@academicstudiespress.com
www.academicstdiespress.com

Contents

Acknowledgements

The authors would like to thank Helena Datner and Agata Patalas for their help in the realization of discussions in Poland. Thanks also to Myra (Steinlauf) Fischer and Ed Fischer for help in discovering and identifying family photographs; to Łukasz Kos for sharing his family photographs; to Michael Sobelman and Yechiel Mordechai Weizman for translating Hebrew epitaphs; and to Anna Engelking and Dorota Leśniewska, Beata Jankowska and Dorota Święcicka for many hours, often unpaid, of dedicated labor on the original Polish version of the text.

Substantive and editorial work: Elżbieta Janicka

Translation into English: Michael Steinlauf

And many thanks to the following for Kickstarter and other support: Deb Sack, Zev Steinlauf, Ben Steinlauf, Gabe Sack, Meri Adelman, Jack LeVert, Cindy Ballenger, Eddy Portnoy, Irene Pletka Kronhill, Sam Kassow, Ellie Kellman, Phyllis Minsky, Tom Hubka, Marc Newman, Stuart Shils, Charlie Miller, Steve Tobias, Tresa Grauer, Avi Kaplan, Agi Legutko, Anna Herman, Robert Dudnick, Paula Parsky, Wolf Krakowski, Jonathan Friedan, Ilana Trachtman, David Sack, Gail Donnelly, Suzanne Alberga, Jeremy Alberga, Allen Tobias, Jonathan Brent, Alyssa Quint, Nikki Marczak, David Mazower, Barbara Kirshenblatt-Gimblett, Karen Underhill, Aaron Lansky, Karen Auerbach, Jan Schwarz, Diana and Don Rothman, Eleanor Shapiro, Joseph Davis, Paul Finkelman, Monika Rice, Glenn Dynner, Ruth Ellen Gruber, David Engel, Ronit Engel, Antony Polonsky, Krzysztof Czyżewski, Adam Zeff, Michael Steiman, Frank London, Pam Pittinger, Paul Cronin, Lara Marks, Jack Kugelmass, Kathryn Hellerstein, Laura Levitt, Donna Allender, Jeffrey Green, Ellen Mains, Hilton Obenzinger, Molly Crabapple, Lisa Mayer, Sruli Dresdner, Marci Shore, Dan Kahn, Ken Parsigian, Walter Laydle, Margaret Olin, Nicholas Croft, Jennifer Egri, Lawrence Rosenwald.

Preface

This book began in 2014 when Elżbieta Janicka approached Michael Steinlauf about the possibility of conducting a long, multifaceted interview with him. Such an endeavor is a Polish genre known as *wywiad-rzeka*, interview-river. Over the following years, Janicka and Steinlauf met in Warsaw, New York and Philadelphia, recorded their conversations, in Polish, and assembled them into a narrative which was published in a journal of the Institute of Slavic Studies of the Polish Academy of Sciences.[1] An expanded version was translated by Steinlauf into English. In your hands or on your screen, dear reader, are the results.

---

1   Elżbieta Janicka, "'To nie była Ameryka.' Z Michaelem Charlesem Steinlaufem rozmawia Elżbieta Janicka (Warszawa – Nowy Jork – Warszawa, 2014–2015)," *Studia Litteraria et Historica*, 2014–15 (3–4), pp. 364–480, https://ispan.waw.pl/journals/index.php/slh/article/view/slh.2015.021.

Chapter 1

Poland, 1980s

Elżbieta Janicka: When did you first come to Poland and what kind of a country was it then?

Michael Steinlauf: It was near the end of martial law. In spring 1983, maybe a bit later. You didn't see tanks anymore, but there were still fully armed three-man patrols in the streets. I spent about twelve months here then in two separate stays. In 1990, I returned for four months more, which makes about sixteen months. The first time, I had a Fulbright Fellowship to research the Polish contexts of the work of Y. L. Peretz, the Yiddish culture hero. But things turned out differently because right away I got to know people in the underground, and among them those who were discovering their Jewishness. This was amazing because in America no one cared much about the past. And so, I began to learn about Jewish things along with Paweł Śpiewak, Helena Datner, Monika and Staszek Krajewski, Kostek Gebert.[1] Ninel Kameraz-Kos, who died not long ago, was really important. I miss her a lot. We would sit around her samovar—it was a real one—and drink tea and vodka. We'd talk all night. No deadlines or alarm clocks. Ninel sang beautifully in Russian, in Yiddish. It was a real bohemia, like from before the counterculture. At any time of the day or night you were a welcome guest, so the house was always filled with people. And it was a place on earth that was totally marked by Jewish things, totally devoted to them. Do you know Ninel's story?

---

1   These were among the founders of the alternative Jewish community in Poland, active culturally and politically in a multitude of ways beginning in the late 1970s with the Jewish Flying University [Żydowski Uniwersytet Latający, ŻUL].

EJ: I only know that she was a painter. She also worked at the Jewish Historical Institute.

MS: She was born in the 1930s in Moscow. Her parents were yiddish-ists.[2] Communists too. Ninel spells Lenin backwards. Her father was arrested on the day she was born. He returned ten years later. After 1956, when it became possible, the whole family decided to leave for Poland. This was popularly referred to as "repatriation." Her husband Bohdan wasn't Jewish. He studied Jewish mysticism, lectured on kab-bala. Ninel lived in Praga [Warsaw neighborhood on the east bank of the Vistula], in a broken-down building that used to belong to the pre-war Jewish community.

EJ: On her grave in the Okopowa cemetery there's a memorial stone to this building, actually to the apartment, to the place: Jagiellońska 28, apartment 1.

Grave of Ninel Kameraz-Kos. The Hebrew inscription reads: "May her soul be bound up in the bond of life." The Polish inscription reads: "We miss you." Jewish cemetery, Okopowa Street, Warsaw, August 2, 2015. Phot. Elżbieta Janicka.

---

2   Yiddishism was a movement that, in its most highly developed form, saw Yiddish as the language of the diaspora Jewish nation, the basis for Jewish demands for state-supported secular cultural autonomy. It emerged in Eastern Europe at the turn of the twentieth century. In Eastern Europe, yiddishists collaborated with the Jewish socialist Bund or the autonomist Yidishe Folkspartey [Folkist Party].

MS: I didn't know. [Silence.] So Ninel was that house. She made things safe. She radiated warmth. For me she was a bit like an older friend, and a bit like a *yidishe mame*. I remember our trip to Tykocin one summer. In a plundered and overgrown Jewish cemetery, Ninel found a *matseyve* [gravestone] adorned with a little horse which she sketched. Besides this, she painted, of course. Somewhat like Grandma Moses. The walls were all hung with her surrealistic Jewish paintings done in that primitivist style. Her younger son Mateusz was the first boy back then to have a bar-mitzvah. Now he's a rabbi in Manchester. The older one, Łukasz, buried himself in Schulz and Kafka, later became a theater director. Various Jews would show up there. From America and not from America. Mainly though from Poland. I discovered a Jewish society there, such a small Jewish world.

Rear of synagogue in Tykocin [Yid. Tiktin]. From the left: Ninel Kameraz-Kos, Mateusz Kos, Michael Steinlauf, Łukasz Kos. Ninel is adjusting the fringes [Yid. *tsitsis*] on Mateusz's *talles kotn* [religious undergarment]. Summer 1983. Copyright Łukasz Kos.

EJ: This was a surprise for you?

MS: Coming here I had no expectations; I didn't imagine anything. I liked everything here. The space, the directness, the sincerity. People sensitive to each other, spending a lot of time together. A big city without a single billboard. I felt that someday there would be nostalgia for this time. The Poles told me I was nuts. No one believed that it would ever change at all. The Soviet Union seemed eternal. As late as 1987, Alina Cała[3] was convinced that the Soviet Empire would last at least two hundred years, and in any case not one of us would see its end. There was a feeling of no way out, of isolation from the world, but at the same time great closeness among people. In addition, I had a thousand-dollar stipend. Do you know what that was then?

EJ: A fortune!

MS: An incredible fortune! I carried those dollars in a special belt. I was the king of Warsaw. I could easily invite four friends to an elegant dinner at Bazyliszek.[4] For a lot of people I was a visitor from another planet, someone with dollars and an American passport.

The atmosphere in Poland was extraordinary. There were anti-government demonstrations that I attended diligently. In Przemyśl, where I found myself with my visiting American girlfriend precisely on the first of May, I was held by the militia for about four hours. I was interrogated by a guy who reminded me of the Grand Inquisitor. I really felt in that police station as though I was in the *Brothers Karamazov*. He tried to explain himself and establish an understanding with me, saying that in every country, including America, there's a need for people like him. But the most important demonstration for me took place a day or two before the official commemoration of the fortieth anniversary of the Warsaw Ghetto Uprising. It was known that the government was planning a very big event, so Solidarity organized a counter-demonstration. Not too many people came, maybe some three hundred. Kostek Gebert

---

3 Cultural anthropologist and historian, scholar of Polish-Jewish relations, feminist activist.
4 Then fanciest restaurant in Warsaw, located in the marketplace of the Old City.

said *kaddish*.[5] This was a little way off from the monument,[6] which itself was surrounded by the ZOMO.[7] I tried to keep to a safe distance because I was afraid of being arrested and deported.

The person I probably learned the most from was the elderly Pan Wróblewski—Andrzej. Pan Wróblewski came from Vilna [Yiddish Vilne, Polish Wilno, Lithuanian Vilnius]. During the war he was in the Polish Socialist Party and generally had nothing to do with Jewish matters. He survived those years on the Aryan side.[8] His autobiography, which came out later, in the '90s, he entitled *Być Żydem* ... [To be a Jew ...]. He lived in Żoliborz [northern Warsaw neighborhood]. I'd come to see him, we'd smoke cigarettes. Strong ones. I don't know if you know them ...

EJ: *Ekstra Mocne.*

MS: Extra Strongs. Terrific, very tasty. We smoked these Extra Strongs, and we drank this really powerful coffee, perhaps five teaspoons of coffee to a little cup.[9] Several of these coffees in the course of a single meeting and nothing to eat. Pan Wróblewski at the time was already in his seventies. We sat, talked on and on, covered everything, and practically every time there would come these indescribable moments. Often it would happen out in the street before or after we talked. Suddenly something would become clear. Ordinary events would take on large meanings,

---

5   The Jewish prayer for the dead, which requires a minimum of ten people to be recited.

6   Nathan Rapoport and Leon Marek Suzin's Warsaw Ghetto Fighters and Martyrs Memorial, erected in 1948, key site for all Polish Holocaust commemorations.

7   Tactical police who wielded long sticks and had a reputation for brutality.

8   That is, living as a Christian Pole and not in any ghetto. EJ notes that removing the quotation marks from the word "Aryan" as well as the phrases "Aryan side" and "Aryan papers," we follow the practice of scholars at the Center for Holocaust Research, Polish Academy of Sciences [Centrum Badań nad Zagładą Żydów, Polska Akademia Nauk] as well as the annual *Zagłada Żydow*. "Even if these expressions were planted into Polish ground by Nazi propaganda, in subsequent years they passed into colloquial use, the best evidence for which are contemporary memoirs, diaries and also the underground press." (Jan Grabowski, *"Ja tego Żyda znam!" Szantażowanie Żydów w Warszawie, 1939–1943* [Warsaw: Wydawnictwo IFiS PAN, 2013], p. 22.) In Polish culture, the reality described by these expressions was a fact before they appeared. See Helena Datner, *Ta i tamta strona. Żydowska inteligencja Warszawy drugiej połowy XIX wieku* (Warsaw: Żydowski Instytut Historyczny, 2007). The popular use of these terms hasn't changed.

9   Poles call such coffee *szatan* [satan].

powerful coincidences, illuminations would emerge. Jung called such moments synchronicities.

And here, I must recall someone even more connected—consciously connected—to such moments. Gayle Wimmer was an American artist I met shortly after I arrived in Poland. She had come to Poland much earlier also on a Fulbright to study with the legendary fiber artist Magda Abakanowicz. Gayle had a small attic apartment from which you could just about touch the roof of the Church of the Redeemer, one of the most magnificent Warsaw churches. This was her base during the months of martial law when the tanks rolled through the streets. Imagine how crazy it was to remain a vegetarian during that time! Gayle managed. And she had set up her loom in that attic and kept working. At a certain moment, she went from weaving rags together to ripping long strips of newspaper and weaving them into "scrolls" large and small. With Gayle synchro-nicities were what life was woven of. In the countryside *bociany* [storks] and *snopki* [mounds of bundled straw] glowed with meaning. Jewish cemeteries and ruined synagogues would appear around the corner. She would encourage things to happen too, regularly placing a spikey bird-of-paradise flower behind the head of a warrior in the Warsaw ghetto monument. "In Poland you just breathe in," she'd say, "then you go back and breathe out." I lost touch with her for a long time, then found out she'd passed away several years ago.

EJ: Łukasz Kos, Ninel's son, discovered a photograph taken in the '80s in front of the Lubomirski Palace in Warsaw in which you're all there—you, Ninel and the boys, the Krajewskis, along with Gayle. He told me what a powerful impression her weavings made on him. And do you know that I met her? In Warsaw. At the end of the 90s. Rapid walk. Diminutive under her backpack and her thick gold braid. Radiant smile. Giant glasses. And finally Gayle. In that order. We met at an exhibit of Jeffrey Wolin's pho-tographs at the Kazimierzowski Palace at the University. Wolin's photo-graphs were of Holocaust survivors. At that time Gayle lived on Lwowska Street. She would invite me to visit, but studies, work, the battle to sur-vive … Neo-liberal capitalism and social Darwinism … I didn't have the time. I regret it. I already regretted it then. I didn't know that she died. I still have her card with the University of Arizona logo. And on the back, carefully lettered: Lwowska 8, apartment 10. And her home phone.

In front of the Lubomirski Palace (left to right front): Małgorzata Krych, Ninel Kameraz-Kos (1937–2011), Łukasz Kos, Gayle Wimmer (1943–2013), Mateusz Kos; left to right rear: Michael Steinlauf, Monika Krajewska, Stanisław Krajewski. Copyright Łukasz Kos.

MS: [Silence.] Getting back to Wróblewski – and another "coincidence." Not far away from his apartment, also in Żoliborz, lived Shloyme Belis-Legis. Also from Vilna. A literary critic. A co-founder and member of the Yiddish literary movement Yung Vilne.[10] We would go see him. He had a Russian wife who took care of him. She served us coffee. Belis arrived in Poland somehow probably in the '60s.

EJ: After '56 at the invitation of the Yiddish newspaper *Folks Shtimme*.

MS: He sat in a Sanacja[11] prison before the war, during the war he fought as a volunteer in the Red Army, in which he enlisted in Samarkand. A

---

10 Yung Vilne (1927–43) was the last of several avant-garde Yiddish literary and artistic movements in interwar Poland. Its participants were mostly on the left politically and identified as yiddishists.

11 Authoritarian political grouping based in the Polish independence movement founded by Józef Piłsudski. It was in power between 1926 and 1939.

tumultuous life. He never learned Polish. His languages were Yiddish and Russian but Pan Wróblewski knew German really well. So Wróblewski spoke to Belis in German and Belis answered him in Yiddish. And that's how they talked. These were unforgettable moments for me. Two old men, both from Vilna, but each from a different world. Wróblewski sleekly Polish. Belis the squat proletarian. Their worlds had nothing in common with each other. Besides, that's the way Miłosz describes it, remembering Vilna.

EJ: I have the book here. *Native Realm*, the chapter called "Nationalities." It's about interwar public education subordinated to the ethno-religious chauvinism of the dominant group. "Such a school, by replacing a many-cultured heritage with national attitudes cut according to the latest fashion, must also have laid the foundations for antisemitism among its pupils. The Jewish religious literature that sprang from this part of Europe was translated into many languages and won recognition all over the world. One has only to pick up the first good anthology of religious thought that comes to hand to run across Hasidic proverbs and to start thinking with respect about the wise men in out-of-the-way small towns [...]. Here, too, later on Yiddish secular prose and poetry were born, with their unique combination of tragedy and inimitable humor. But we, in the very city where those books were printed, knew literally nothing about them. Several fell into my hands many years later when I bought them in New York—I had to learn English in order to make contact with something that had been only an arm's length away."[12]

MS: Precisely.

EJ: What were the discussions between Wróblewski and Belis-Legis about?

MS: I don't remember exactly. They talked about Vilna, the war, literary matters. I regret that I didn't take notes then. I also went off with Pan Wróblewski to Wrocław where Jakób Rotbaum [Yankev Rotboym], the great Yiddish theater director, lived. His sister Lea Rotbaum danced in

---

12 Czesław Miłosz, *Native Realm,* trans. by Catherine S. Leach (New York: Farrar, Straus, and Giroux, 2002), p. 98.

Russia in the '30s, later became a choreographer and opera director. We visited them in a huge dark old apartment. Rotbaum sat at an enormous table. Wróblewski conducted an interview with him. I don't know what became of those tapes. Jakób and Lea died in the same year, in the mid-90s. Briefly, Wróblewski, who never had anything to do with Jews, introduced me into Jewishness. He understood that a young Jew had arrived here looking for something. Something. He goes to Okopowa [Jewish cemetery], meanders among the gravestones. Wróblewski understood. The last time I saw him was in the '90s. He had cancer already then, but he said that with a tough hide like his it could take a while. And, in fact, he lived to be eighty-five.

EJ: Wróblewski never had anything to do with Jewish matters except for the fact that he was subjected to antisemitic violence. For fear of his safety, he never returned to his prewar name, something which today his grandson has his nose rubbed into. The book *To Be a Jew ...* is dedicated

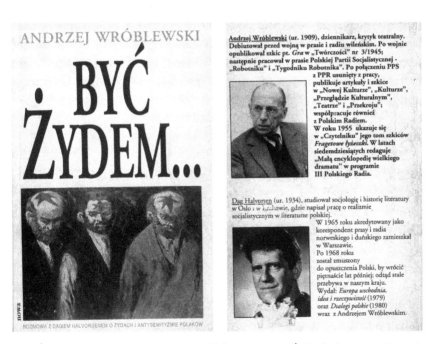

Być Żydem ... Rozmowa z Dagiem Halvorsenem o Żydach i antysemityzmie Polaków [To be a Jew ...: A Conversation with Dag Halvorsen about Jews and Poles' Antisemitism] (Warsaw: Niezależna Oficyna Wydawnicza, 1992). On the cover: Branded by Mark Oberländer, 1955. Phot. Elżbieta Janicka.

to "Anna—my Aryan wife." It was published in 1992 with a reproduction of Marek Oberländer's painting *Branded* on the cover, and met with a warm welcome from the Polish radical right, from the historian Jerzy Robert Nowak, for example, who denies Polish crimes against Jews. How to understand this? Because I read this book as a story about the price of assimilation—or acculturation—into an antisemitic culture.

MS: Subjected to antisemitic violence? That's a bit strong. During the Occupation, Wróblewski worked in the Polish underground and survived. He succeeded in functioning as a Pole because he identified as a Pole, so he didn't take part in what Grynberg called the Jewish war.[13]

EJ: Where there's a will there's a way.

MS: In his case it really worked. I can't reproach him for that. In his book, it's true, he seems not to understand antisemitism, sets up some kind of symmetry between Jews and Poles. In the context of Polish-Jewish relations, he recommends the evangelical stance of "We forgive and ask for forgiveness." I understand that this is where the raves of the radical right come from. Nevertheless, it was this man who later sought Jewishness and helped me find myself in Poland in 1983.

EJ: Sandauer was also important for you.

MS: Oh yes. When I first arrived in Warsaw, I lived at the Grand Hotel on Krucza Street, today the Mercure. Back then it was a typical Stalinist monster. I'll never forget how I sat in my hotel room and read Sandauer's little book *O sytuacji pisarza polskiego pochodzenia żydowskiego w XX wieku. Rzecz, którą nie ja powinienem był napisać ...* [On the situation of the Jewish writer of Polish descent in the twentieth century: it is not I who should have written this study...].[14] Terrific text. Published in 1982 by the state publishing house Czytelnik just before my arrival. I was fascinated. A new world opened before me. I learned about writers previously

---

13 See Henryk Grynberg, *The Jewish War* and *The Victory*, trans. by Richard Lourie and Celina Wieniewska (Chicago: Northwestern University Press, 2001).

14 Artur Sandauer (1913–89); English translation by Abe Shenitzer and Sara Shenitzer (Jerusalem: Magnes Press, 2005).

unknown to me and their struggles with their own identity. It was the first thing in my life that I read in Polish. I laboriously deciphered the letters, then put them together and sounded the word out. In order to understand I had to read out loud. Because I knew Polish, of course, only as a spoken language. I'd never seen the Polish alphabet before, with all those diacritical marks. I didn't know anything about punctuation, spelling. Every minute I had to look up some word in the dictionary that I didn't know from home. An amazing experience. Instant literacy. But when I told my new Jewish friends about my reading, they rebuffed me with "Sanduaer is a collaborator." Simply that. Without a word of commentary. In contrast to them, Sandauer wasn't boycotting the government. I didn't understand why I should judge a book on the basis of the political choices of its author. But I should have remembered my Marxist years, when there were lots of artists and writers, Saul Bellow for instance, who were considered "bourgeois." Today we'd say "politically incorrect."

EJ: What it was about is that after martial law was declared, Sandauer joined the National Council of Culture, which supported [General] Jaruzelski.[15] But he didn't do it to conform. He never belonged to the ruling party [Polish United Workers' Party – Polska Zjednoczona Partia Robotnicza, PZPR]. At the end of the '40s, when courage didn't come cheap, he openly fought socialist realism. He was punished for this by a ban on the publication of his works. He was the first writer who, living in Poland, dared to publish under his own name in the Parisian [émigré] journal *Kultura*. In the '50s and '60s he fought for recognition for Gombrowicz.[16] In 1964, he signed an open letter of thirty-four intellectuals to the president of the Council of Ministers against tightening censorship. He saw Solidarity as a foreshadowing of what today is called restoration of Polishness, which threatened his sense of safety and the values he stood for. It's interesting that he was considered a collaborator by those who were themselves ready to collaborate with a force—as we see today—more powerful than one or another general or system.

MS: What do you mean?

---

15 It was Wojciech Jaruzelski who had declared martial law in December 1981.

16 Witold Gombrowicz (1904–69), Polish avant-garde writer and playwright whose works were banned in the early years of postwar communism.

EJ: I mean Polish culture and society. In the essay in question, Sandauer exposed the violence of the dominant culture in relation to Jews; he wrote about minority identity under the extreme pressure of the majority. He steamrolled over Ficowski. He rolled over Słonimski, who was dear to Adam Michnik.[17] These were all icons of the opposition. He didn't leave the Polish intelligentsia, in their relationship to Jews, a leg to stand on. This for instance: "That unclear feeling that Jews are both for good and for ill something exceptional, has begun to develop—especially among the young intelligentsia sensitive to trends. The rarity of the Jew, his exoticism, becomes a lure that's nearly erotic. Most postwar statements on this subject are characterized by a sentimental exaltation; that also applies to critical assessments of works on the subject."[18] Or: "Popular particularly among the intelligentsia, philosemitism [...] is neverthe-less still cultivated—as we will see—in a medium of imaginings that are allo—or completely antisemitic."[19] Independent of our judgment of Sandauer's political options after 1980, these thoughts devastated all the delicate identity acrobatics of the "new Jews."

MS: He certainly didn't seem apologetic. Later I discovered that still in the '50s he was one of the first to write about Bruno Schulz. But in the '80s, in oppositional circles, you were only allowed to read kosher Ficowski but not *treyf* Sandauer.

---

17 Jerzy Ficowski (1924–2006) and Antoni Słonimski (1895–1976) were poets, both identified with the "Polish recovery of Jewish memory." Michnik (b. 1946) was a leader of the Polish democratic opposition who became editor-in-chief of *Gazeta Wyborcza*, the liberal Polish daily. Bruno Schulz (1892–1942) was a Polish-Jewish writer and artist who Isaac Bashevis Singer described as a cross between Proust and Kafka. He was murdered by a Nazi officer in the Drohobycz ghetto. Sandauer and Ficowski were the key figures in Schulz's rediscovery in postwar Poland. They both first wrote about him in 1956. Sandauer's essay was published as the introduction to Schulz's first postwar collection of writings, *Proza* (Kraków: Wydawnictwo Literackie, 1964); Ficowski later wrote a biography that's been translated into English as *Regions of the Great Heresy: Bruno Schulz, A Biographical Portrait*, trans. by Theodosia S. Robertson (New York: Norton, 2003).

18 *On the situation of the Polish writer of Jewish descent in the twentieth century: it is not I who should have written this study...*, p. 75.

19 *On the situation*, p. 87. The term "allo-semitism," coined by Sandauer, refers to fascination with Jews either positively or negatively, that is, either philo- or anti-semitism. Here we've chosen to dispense with the hyphens.

Monthly Warsaw public transportation pass with photograph of Michael Steinlauf, 1983. Copyright Michael Steinlauf.

EJ: Did you ever expect that the Soviet Union would fall?

MS: No. I thought about it sometimes, but probably no one either within the system or outside it had any real notion of just how flimsy it was.

EJ: Because they always remembered the war and even Afghanistan couldn't shake the story of the unconquered Red Army. Besides, all this rot could just as well have become a chronic condition and lasted despite everything for a long time still, with blood spilled and other paroxysms. But I'm interested in what you thought of Solidarity.

MS: I'll say it briefly. Arriving in Poland, I was a big leftist. I return to America and tell my friends: "Listen, in Poland it's exactly like it was here, except that their greatest heroes are the Pope and Ronald Reagan." You can imagine how this went down. Everyone thought I'd gone nuts.

Strange how all this intersected, because when in 1988 the Krajewskis were in New York, I brought them to the twenty-year commemoration of the Columbia sit-ins. In 1968, we took over the university, there were battles with the police, kind of an uprising. And Staszek says weren't we supporters of everything he and his friends fought against in 1968. That not one of us expressed open solidarity with Czechoslovakia. But later Staszek adds: "So why do I feel so good among these supporters of communism?" Because he really felt totally at home then at Columbia. The same faces, the same jeans, the same way people related to each other.

EJ: It pained him that none of you supported Czechoslovakia, but it didn't pain him that none of you, just like none of them, supported the persecuted Polish Jews in the same year.

MS: You weren't there. 1968 was a moment of international solidarity of young people. Young people ruled above and beyond politics and they knew it. But quickly everything returned to "adult" norms. And to answer your question about Solidarity: I didn't take in everything, of course. I didn't know any workers, but I felt very close to the Solidarity intelligentsia. Columbia and Solidarity were in some sense similar.

EJ: I understand that what Columbia and Solidarity—or more generally America of the '60s and Solidarity—were supposed to have had in common was a struggle for emancipation. So, in that case, what was with Reagan and the Pope?

MS: Solidarity was created by people who went through 1968.

EJ: In the sense you mean, not so much Solidarity as KOR.[20] And it was '68 in Poland with all its national-conservative reclamation. "Zionists to Siam" on one side, on the other, *Forefathers' Eve* and "independence without censorship."[21] Both sides shared a common assumption; the struggle between them was about who better represented the "Polish soul." In other words, this was a struggle for legitimacy within a common paradigm.

MS: I completely disagree.

---

20 Workers' Defense Committee [Komitet Obrony Robotników, KOR] which came out of strikes in 1976.

21 The slogan "Zionists to Siam [Syjoniści do Syjamu]" which appeared on some placards in 1967–68 was based on an ignorant and comical misunderstanding. Where would *Syjoniści* [Seeyonishchi] go but to Seeyam, that is, Siam? On the other side, the banning of a production of Adam Mickiewicz's nineteenth century play *Forefathers' Eve*, a cornerstone of the Polish national mythos, was the spark that set off student demonstrations in those years. "Independence without censorship" was a student slogan.

EJ: Grzegorz Niziołek in his study *The Polish Theatre of the Holocaust* explains that in the '60s in Polish high culture the mocking revision of Romantic myths established no alternative order, but empowered a "model of cultural victimhood shaped by Romanticism" that was strongly aroused by the war experience. What emerged was a "self-perpetuating closed circuit [...] (advantageous for the defensive mechanisms of the collective libido) [...]." "The object of profoundest denial" was not national mythology but "an experience that had become part of Polish society's recent past was therefore negated and suppressed."[22] What concerns Niziołek is the Polish experience of the Holocaust, and therefore also antisemitism. What sort of emancipation and whose are we talking about, since in 1968 Jews were traditionally clobbered and no one said a word?[23]

MS: Yet I don't agree that '68 was only formative for KOR. And I say this based on personal experience, and not based on books. Important is what one lives through, not just what one reads. All those I met and spent time with in the '80s were underground activists, mainly Jews, and all had been previously active in '68. Indeed, just like Michnik himself. For me and for other young people there was something in the experiences of '68 that transcended local politics. Once, many years later, I said that at this moment we felt the rustling of the skirts of Messiah. He came close,

---

22 Trans. by Ursula Phillips (London: Methuen, 2019), pp. 35–36. In Polish, see *Polski teatr Zagłady* (Warsaw: Instytut Teatralny im. Zbigniewa Raszewskiego and Wydawnictwo Krytyki Politycznej, 2013), pp. 62–63.

23 EJ notes that this issue reappeared at the time of the installation of the permanent exhibition at the Museum of the History of Polish Jews in Warsaw. Government officials complained to the authors of the postwar gallery, Helena Datner and Stanisław Krajewski. "We discussed whether there were too few student leaflets shown condemning antisemitism. But I don't remember that there were very many. Usually what's condemned in them is both antisemitism and Zionism, the typical line of contemporary propaganda. There were perhaps one or two, including from my own philosophy department, in which only antisemitism was condemned. Defending Jewish comrades was not something that engaged the student movement at the time. It was a struggle about free speech, a sort of political counterculture. It wasn't an antisemitic movement, like part of Solidarity later on, it just focused on something else; it didn't notice the Jewish problem" ("Datner: Żydowski punkt widzenia. Pyta Kacha Szaniawska [Rozmowa]," *Krytyka Polityczna*, May 30, 2015, http://www.krytykapolityczna.pl/artykuly/historia/20150529/datner-zydowski-punkt-widzenia-rozmowa).

made his presence known, reminded us of himself with the lightest of touches, and that's it, he was gone. Walter Benjamin in his last writings suggested something like this.[24]

EJ: Let's return to Reagan and the Pope. After all, even omitting personal details, authority and emancipation exclude each other.

MS: Not always. Che Guevara? But then Reagan spoke of the Soviet Union as the Evil Empire, this really spoke to the imagination. Arriving in Poland, I supported the idea that there were two evil empires: the Soviet Union and the U.S. Yet after some time in Poland, I concluded that you couldn't compare the two.

EJ: And this after the destruction by the United States of the world monetary order, which the United States itself established in 1944 at Bretton Woods, accepting the principle of the redeemability of the dollar for gold? This was the beginning of the worldwide chaos in financial markets. 1971. The real economy began to collide increasingly with virtual financial operations. As a result, we got the catastrophe of 2008 and its continuation, which we live in, and which no one is capable of overcoming. Perhaps an intellectual shouldn't accept as his vision of the world something out of intellectually black-and-white action films, such as Darth Vader vs. Luke Skywalker. Soviet domination of Poland was more terrible than American domination in South America, as I understand it? Or is it a question of the left-wing idea in general?

---

24 "The past carries with it a temporal index by which it is referred to redemption. There is a secret agreement between past generations and the present one. Our coming was expected on earth. Like every generation before us, we have been endowed with a *weak* messianic power, a power to which the past has a claim. That claim cannot be settled cheaply [...]. The true picture of the past flits by. The past can be seized only as an image which flashes up at the instant when it can be recognized and is never seen again [...]. For every image of the past that is not recognized by the present as one of its own concerns threatens to disappear irretrievably." And there is also this, more concretely: "In every era the attempt must be made anew to wrest tradition away from a conformism that is about to overpower it" ("Theses on the Philosophy of History," in *Illuminations: Essays and Reflections*, trans. by Harry Zohn, [New York: Schocken, 1969], pp. 254–55). EJ questions whether the generation of '68 met Benjamin's redemptive criterion and suggests that this sentence contains the kernel of our present dispute.

MS: Popular culture has a lot to offer. And this is something that Polish intellectuals can learn from Americans. In the United States, there have been serious studies of popular culture for a long time now. As for the crash of 2008, I'll remind you that the United States has recovered. In contrast to Europe. And the left-wing idea hasn't worked out.

EJ: But it worked out well with the accumulation of capital which doesn't have to worry about liberal democracy or other nonsense such as social justice for instance.

MS: Agreed. I was and I still am on the left. But I don't know if the kind of transformation of relations that Marx wrote about in the *1844 Manuscripts* is possible. I saw the contradictions. The Pope was a great figure then in Poland. I knew that the same person in South America undermined popular movements and legitimized oppression. But here in Poland, what was terrific is that he coopted the communists' own slogans. How do you say it? *Godność pracy*?

EJ: Yes. Dignity of labor.

MS: That was amazing.

EJ: But it was a hostile takeover. Intended against the idea of emancipation, blocking its very possibility. Everyone or nearly everyone got excited that one power was whacking another power, one hierarchy another, our boys over the Ruskies. But very few—if anyone at all—noticed the nationalism and the reactionary charge in Wojtyła's message. Not to mention his notions of gender. I have in mind all those winged words about the dignity of woman, about her calling to virginity and motherhood. In postwar public discourse, this had no precedent, but no one noticed, and even if they did, they preferred to remain silent. Along with Michnik's book,[25] it was not the Church that was changing, but the Left that acceded to its own liquidation.

---

25 *The Church, the Left, Dialogue,* translated by Jan T. Gross (Chicago: University of Chicago Press, 1993). The original, *Kościół, lewica, dialog,* was published in 1977.

MS: At the time this was hardly visible, and not just for me. What was most important back then was the struggle against state power. After reading Michnik, it seemed after all that the Church was changing, that its national-conservative stance was becoming less important.

EJ: Less important under the wings of the Pope who destroyed liberation theology? Wojtyła of Chile and Wojtyła of Poland was the same Wojtyła. There was no conflict between them.

MS: Notice that the Church back then didn't endorse slogans that were openly confrontational, nor did they oppose a project in which there would be a place for everyone. One could believe, delude oneself perhaps, that it was a different institution. And yet … on the thirteenth of every month in all churches, special masses were held to remember those who were still interned. I rarely missed one. The Church after all was the ally of the opposition, and this at the most difficult moments. I usually went to Holy Cross Church on Krakowskie Przedmieście opposite the University. During the mass, opposition leaflets would rain down from the balcony and everyone would gather them up. Me too. Besides this, I stood like the others and kneeled. In order to show respect. I would choose a spot a bit further back, not far from the door. One time I'm kneeling, and I notice directly in front of me, on the side of a pew, a small plaque in honor of Roman Dmowski,[26] and I feel—literally, physically feel—how at that very moment in the Okopowa Cemetery my grandfathers, great-grandfathers and the rest of the family are turning in their graves. I jumped to my feet as though burned. I'll never forget it. So, I had moments of doubt. A good number of such moments. I somehow understood that at some point the Church would return to being that old Church. And that's exactly what happened. But in general, these were amazing times, awesome times.

EJ: In 1990 was it still so awesome?

---

26 Roman Dmowski (1864–1939) was the founder and leader of the antisemitic National Democratic Party [Narodowa Demokracja, ND or Endecja]. The present Law and Justice Party [Prawo i Sprawiedliwość, PiS], which rules in today's Poland, is the heir of Dmowski's ideas. Its antisemitism is more veiled, however.

MS: I returned then for four months. Hoping to get back to Poland, I first went to Washington where the U.S. Holocaust Memorial Museum was being planned and got myself sent to Poland in order to investigate the situation of Holocaust-era archives. And this already was a different Poland. I arrive, look around, and see a pickup truck with its tailgate down. On one side, stacks of raw meat piled on newspapers, on the other side, copies of the *Protocols of the Elders of Zion*. The stuff most immediately needed, you understand.

EJ: What did you think then?

MS: I thought that the country was in the throes of vast change, and that everything that was hidden before was seeping out into the light of day.

EJ: Did you perceive this as transformation or rather as re-creation, restoration?

MS: First for me was always the Jewish perspective. As in 1983. That someone found some *siddur* [prayer book] and showed it to me. Or discovered a neglected cemetery or synagogue and led me there. What the Krajewskis did.[27] This was what was fundamental and most important for me. History as something sacred.

EJ: And how was that sacredness supposed to find itself among Reagan, the Pope, and the *Protocols of the Elders of Zion*? Did you consider how the majority culture, about which you weren't uncritical after all, was going to relate to it?

MS: I reflected. The result was that I gave up my studies of Peretz for the time being and decided to tell about what was happening here—as a

---

27 Beginning in the 1970s, Monika and Stanisław Krajewski wandered throughout Poland documenting plundered Jewish cemeteries. Monika's photographs were first published as *Czas Kamieni* [A time of stones] (Warsaw: Interpress, 1982) and again as *A Tribe of Stones: Jewish Cemeteries in Poland*, trans. by Kent Bosley and Krystyna Wandycz, introd. by Rafael Scharf (Warsaw: Polish Scientific Publishers, 1993).

spectator, an outside observer.[28] And in Poland itself at that time, in 1990, I didn't feel so good. Being a Jew in that situation was not right somehow … The streets looked a little strange. There was a rather unpleasant, quite unpleasant, really, very unpleasant atmosphere.

EJ: Concretely?

MS: Antisemitism. Openly. Everywhere. Conversations in public places, "Jews to the gas!" graffiti, and so on. I lived in Mokotów [southern Warsaw neighborhood] in a building where Jewish communists once lived. That kind of graffiti was next to the elevator. It was on every side, also professionally.[29] In the archives I talked with monsters still there from the old system. I don't remember names.

EJ: What did you talk about?

MS: Professional matters, contents of the archives, possibilities for accessing them, regular stuff. I realized I'd get nowhere this way and that this work had to be done by a Pole, at least someone who lived here. And I had a close friend, the first person, actually, who I met in Poland, because back in 1983 he came to get me at the airport. This was Jerzy Halbersztadt. He was always a little different, a little on the side. He had a different take on Solidarity. It wasn't so simple for him.

EJ: He saw it critically?

MS: In any case he wasn't an uncritical fan of Solidarity and that's why some of my other friends, like the Krajewskis, didn't want to have much to do with him. I proposed Jerzy [Jurek] as the permanent representative of the Holocaust Museum in Washington and this turned out to be perfect for him and for the museum. Jurek not only handled the archives

---

28 The result was *Bondage to the Dead: Poland and the Memory of the Holocaust* (Syracuse University Press, 1997).

29 "Those stars of David on gallows, the graffiti 'Jews to the gas' […] and this rubs into us after the holy epoch of Solidarity" (letter of Helena Eilstein to Leszek Kołakowski, 1991, cited in Magdalena Grochowska, "Przyjaciółka rozumu," *Gazeta Wyborcza*, August 22–23, 2015, p. 34.

but became the go-to person for the museum people when they came to Warsaw. Later, Shaike Weinberg got to know him. Shaike was the creator of the Diaspora Museum [Beit Hatfutsot] in Tel Aviv, then the Holocaust Museum in Washington—in other words, Jewish historical narrative museums. Weinberg was the first in this field. He was born in Warsaw, raised in Germany, and after Hitler came to power, he made it to Palestine where he served in the Haganah. He convinced Jurek that it was necessary to build something like Beit Hatfutsot in Poland: not a museum of the Holocaust but a museum of the history of Jews. And Jurek became director of the Museum of the History of Polish Jews (Muzeum Historii Żydów Polskich, MHŻP). Shaike died in 2000. To the end he was very concerned about the MHŻP.

EJ: In his *New York Times* obituary, Irvin Molotsky wrote: "At his death, even while slowed by vascular illness, Mr. Weinberg was working on the design of Jewish museums in Warsaw and Berlin."[30] It's curious, because the current leadership of the MHŻP doesn't like to acknowledge Weinberg's role, nor Halbersztadt's for that matter.

MS: In those years, Jurek and I were close friends. He often said that it was through me that he discovered Jewishness, because earlier he was far from such things, knew little about them. You can imagine, communist parents.

EJ: In the '80s in Poland there wouldn't have been anyone discovering Jewishness if not for communist parents, so there's no need to emphasize this precisely in the case of Jerzy Halbersztadt. In Poland it's not a statement of fact but a denunciation.

MS: Still? You're serious? But this is antisemitic!

EJ: Of course it is, but it's not taken as such.

---

30 https://www.nytimes.com/2000/01/04/us/jeshajahu-weinberg-81-led-jewish-museums.html

MS: In any case, Jurek and I talked a great deal about this museum. Jurek felt that he lacked the competence to create the permanent exhibit. So, I recommended a person equally competent in the field of Yiddish culture and museology, and that was Barbara Kirshenblatt-Gimblett.[31] And that's what happened. Barbara became the curator of the permanent exhibit of the MHŻP, a powerful force in its creation.

---

31 At the time, she was the chair of Performance Studies at New York University.

Chapter 2

Columbia, 1960s

EJ: Columbia University, the '60s. What's happening then in America? What's happening in the world?

MS: What's happening? Insurrection in the air. The earth shakes. It seemed to us that an old world was ending and a new one beginning. And that it was in our power to found that new world. That after us social relations would completely change. That capitalism would end once and for all. I really thought that.

EJ: What ideas led you?

MS: We drew from Marx. It was about uniting American and Third World youth, our liberation and yours.[1] We were led by feelings of brotherhood and community, opposition to inequality, exclusion, exploitation, capitalism, racism. We were concerned about universal things, not the narrowly understood interests of our own group. I experienced feelings of unity, of being part of a great whole.

EJ: What kind of environment was it? What kind of people?

MS: The protests, as a whole, were led by a group called SDS—Students for a Democratic Society, but events had a mass character. At a certain moment, we took over much of the university including the main

---

1   A reference to the slogan "For our freedom and yours [*Za naszą i waszą wolność*]" originating amidst the Polish uprisings of the nineteenth century.

administration building. We shut down the classrooms and began an occupation. We were concerned about two issues. Firstly, we demanded the end of any involvement by the university in helping wage the war in Vietnam. Secondly, we protested plans to build a gymnasium near the campus that would have a rear entrance for people from Harlem. We were fighting racism and racist architecture. That's what our principles looked like.

Several years earlier, in 1964 or '65, before the mass protests at Columbia, I'd been a member of CORE [Congress of Racial Equality]. We organized various actions to draw attention to what we considered important matters. Just as I was guarding some people who were on a hunger strike against racism, two elderly people resembling East European intelligentsia appeared on campus. Short, dressed in old-fashioned clothing. And these arrivals from another planet are looking for Steinlauf, for me, in other words. I look and it's my parents. For elderly folks, they were actually quite young, not much over fifty. They came to save me. My father avoided politics his entire life. He was strongly against my involvement. He would repeat that in the United States, for the first time in his life, he felt himself to be a full citizen and in general a human being. He believed that this country deserved loyalty and not revolution. Our relations were awful. The smallest things were excuses for terrible conflicts between us. Today, when I have tense relations with my own seventeen-year-old son, my partner Deborah repeats: "What you gave your father you're getting back now." So, relations with my father were very bad, and my mother ... both of them had survived somewhat worse things than that, but here it was about their kid, about me, so you can imagine. I didn't think about this much back then.

As long as we're talking about the years before '68, another pretty important memory comes to mind. In the summer of 1966—the summer before the "summer of love"—I'd gone to California, to Berkeley, supposedly to summer school. I never went to a single class, but I did start doing acid. And I remember riding down Route 1 along the California coast in the back of a pickup truck after some amazing trips, leaning back with the sun in my face, and thinking "Should I stay here or go back?" I thought about a timeless life living on California beaches. Pretty seductive. But then I distinctly remember a moment when something in me said no. That is, I felt, finally, that I belonged to history, to time, to the East and not the West. It's like the scales moved and I chose history. So I went back. Half a year later, in February '67, my father died and that was that. I had to stay for my mother. But I've thought about that moment in the pickup many times since. It was history clawing its way out, my own history, my parents' history, Jewish history.

But back to Columbia. At the time of the strike, Tom Hayden appeared on campus dressed in a karate gi. He was no longer a student then, but a well-known SDS activist. And he came precisely to us, to Math Hall, which had been taken by the left of the left—*le rouge du rouge*—and I was in this group. I wasn't a leader, but I was certainly with the most radical ones. University officials were especially afraid of what they called "people from outside" coming onto campus. This fear was shared by a portion of the students. It was about people from Harlem, though not only. Because suddenly a group of about six white guys dressed all in black leather appeared at Math Hall. One of them even wore a black leather cowboy hat. They called themselves the Motherfuckers of the Lower East Side.

Occupied Math Hall, April 1968. Food basket on the right. Copyright Columbia University. Used with permission.

Occupied Math Hall, April 1968. Michael Steinlauf in center. Copyright Columbia University. Used with permission.

Marching down College Walk c. May 1968. Michael Steinlauf with clipboard on right. Copyright Columbia University. Used with permission.

EJ: "Wall Street is War Street." "All you need is dynamite."

MS: Yeah, it was them. "A street gang with analysis." They carried knives.

EJ: Anarchists?

MS: Absolutely. Kind of like a self-defense squad, but actually a group of provocateurs coming out of the visual arts and drawing on the tradition of dadaism.

EJ: A word more about the name, whose full version was Up Against the Wall Motherfuckers—from a poem by Amiri Baraka entitled "Black People!"[2] Until meeting up with you all in April '68, they were known as Black Mask. In May, they went underground and the change of name to something obscene also came out of their resistance to being easily consumed. Baraka's poem somehow accompanied your protest, since it first appeared as graffiti on the wall of Math Hall, and later Mark Rudd, the leader of the whole sit-in, cited it at the end of his letter to the president of Columbia.

MS: I really liked Baraka's work. Unfortunately, there was antisemitic stuff in it. He would call for attacks on Jewish stores which there were lots of in black neighborhoods, and he would also demand "Jews, turn in your gold!" At the same time, he was important because on the one hand, he linked us to the Beat Generation and, on the other hand, to the Black Power movement. The Motherfuckers were also an important part of all this. Without their intensity and their ideas things wouldn't have been the same.

EJ: Ginsberg said there was no Beat Generation, just a few guys looking for a publisher.

---

2   "... All the stores will open if you will say the words. The magic words are: Up against the wall mother fucker / this is a stick up! Or: Smash the window at night (these are magic actions) smash the windows daytime, anytime, together, / let's smash the window drag the shit from in there. No money / down. No time to pay. Just take what you want. The magic dance in the street ..." (*Black Magic: Collected Poetry 1961–1967* [Indianapolis and New York: Bobbs-Merrill, 1969], p. 225).

MS: And it all hangs together because Baraka published them. About a week after the start of the strike, the police burst onto campus and in one night arrested seven hundred people. I was in Math Hall with Paul Auster. We were friends then. There were two girls with us. We locked ourselves in one of the offices and waited. We felt they'd come in. We sat on the floor with our arms locked. The police were really brutal and mad at us, because we'd built giant barricades, a whole system of fortifications. And we'd also soaped the stairs, so they lost their balance and fell. And when they got to us, we didn't want to get up. So I got a nightstick in the head which later in the hospital required four stitches. It didn't take long for all of us to jump up and have the police take us out. I'm covered in blood, really proud. Outside—it's insane. Seven hundred people arrested. And people from all over the city who've come to support us are chanting "The whole world is watching." The police are pushing us into paddy wagons. People are trying to get us out. They're rocking the paddy wagons. There's fighting. We're not alone. An amazing feeling, unforgettable. I spent the night in jail. Later, they released us. For me Solidarity was a continuation of that revolt.

EJ: Really? But Solidarity didn't care about the fate of those persecuted in Latin America or elsewhere. Even in the days, unwillingly remembered later on, when it advanced the slogan "Socialism yes, perversion no."

Solidarność logo by Jerzy Janiszewski. Copyright NSZZ "Solidarność." Used with permission.

Don't forget that the logo of Solidarity was, certainly, writing in red. But above this writing was the red-and-white Polish flag. You could see with your naked eye that a lot of solidarity wouldn't come out of this.

MS: Agreed. If you're talking about the evolution of ideology and social practice, it's hard to speak of a resemblance. But it was a similar kind of collective experience, typical of a moment when historic change happens. When the '60s came to an end, such things no longer occurred in America, so I felt really fortunate that I could experience them in Poland. I experienced something similar back in 1967 during the March on Washington. I took part in it actually by accident, because I stumbled across the police, who were keeping people from going in a certain direction, and since they were, I found a way around them. And I found the people who were putting flowers in the soldiers' gun barrels. Powerful experience. In relation to this event a huge role was played by Norman Mailer's book *The Steps of the Pentagon*, a text that in its time was enormously influential.

EJ: I'm trying to understand. Important for you is the type of experience. But an idea or ideology, a stated purpose or goal?

MS: But it was about freedom, about abolishing a system of unfreedom. And other matters? For me in any case at that time in Poland maybe they didn't count for that much. But the question of goals is a tough one. Because what happened in Poland ultimately? And did it work out any better in America? Ronald Reagan came out of this. Ronald Reagan, who was a monster, you understand?

EJ: But it wasn't the sit-in at Columbia that brought Ronald Reagan to power. Your program never included a neo-liberal revolution, not did you support one. Critical thought at Columbia still exists. Thanks to it, we don't live in the "best of worlds," in a world without alternatives. Thanks to those like you, consent to what goes on is not complete.

MS: But we shouldn't forget though that it was fear of what we represented that pushed America into Reagan's embrace. Though in our own estimation we were fighting for a wonderful new world.

EJ: But Solidarity, with its charismatic leader, Lech Wałęsa, very quickly started to fight for the wonderful old world.

MS: It seemed it was enough to overthrow all the communists who were guilty of everything.

EJ: Based on such a definition of the situation one could predict how things would go. You didn't have to be clairvoyant. I'm simplifying a bit, because not everyone reasoned this way, but it wasn't they who steered the sequel.[3] But let's return to Columbia. Who else dropped by? Ginsberg? Aptheker?

MS: I don't remember either of them, but it's certain that both supported us. At the moment we're speaking of, the most important for us was Tom Hayden. Our commune in Math Hall—about a hundred people— elected him chairman. And very important were people from Harlem, who appeared among the students. Blacks, of course, were students at Columbia. A handful. Very intense. They had great ideas, invited various activists. We agreed to occupy adjoining buildings. But what I'm speaking of here are Blacks from the city. I remember them marching down the center of campus. "Bang bang, boom, boom, Ungawa, Black power!" Marvelous story. Less marvelous was the existence on campus of various strongly right-wing fraternities. One of the worst was Beta Theta Pi (they were all named with letters of the Greek alphabet). They were all located

---

3   EJ notes that there is clear research on the rivalry between class interests and democratic ideas, on the one hand, and national-Catholic elements, on the other. "There is no question that the workers fully shared the feelings of Wałęsa when he said: 'The interests of the Polish nation will stand above our own interests' [that is, above class interests ...]. The most important fact is the presence of the Church and of the Catholic religion in Polish national consciousness as well as in the activity of Solidarity. It is in this respect that the failure of Western opinion to understand Poles is the most striking" (Alain Touraine et al., *Solidarność. Analiza ruchu społecznego 1980–1981* [Warsaw: Wydawnictwo Europa, 1989], p. 47). Models of the movement advanced by this team of sociologists evolved. About their final form, Touraine writes: "What they have in common is that they all reduce the importance of the democratic dimension and ascribe a central role to national feelings" (Touraine, p. 145). See also Sergiusz Kowalski, *Krytyka solidarnościowego rozumu. Studium z socjologii myślenia potocznego* (Warsaw: PEN, 1990); and David Ost, *The Defeat of Solidarity: Anger and Politics in Post-Communist Europe* (Ithaca: Cornell University Press, 2005).

on one street, many of the members were athletes, whereas we were supposed to be wimps, a laughingstock for them. They would jump us and beat us up, until one day some guys from Harlem demolished some frat houses in our defense. All this was outdoors, so everyone could watch, since it was warm already, late spring, early summer. After that, the frat boys lost their desire for fighting. From this point on, they were the ones who were afraid. The whites. Scary guests you couldn't talk to. Since they were racists, the myth of Harlem additionally worked on them, which meant we were safe even when the folks from there weren't around.

EJ: Was SDS differentiated internally?

MS: Absolutely. There were socialists, communists, anarchists, liberals of various flavors. We couldn't stand the liberals who wanted to reach some kind of understanding with the administration. Some buildings were occupied by radicals, others by liberals. The result was that the president of Columbia resigned. The planned gymnasium was never built. For years affirmative action became the rule in the recruitment of students and the hiring of university administration as well as faculty, though not long ago the Supreme Court, recently rather right-wing, declared it unconstitutional. To this day, the place where somehow the memory of our sit-in still lives is the administration building. The sit-in became part of the tradition and the identity of the university, part of the legend, but also part of the system of reference. A kind of bogeyman. When my partner Deborah and I first met, we loved the coincidence—synchronicity? — that she worked in the Columbia administration, in Low Library, where the memory of '68 was still alive. In sum, I'd say that Columbia changed, but in the way the liberals wanted it. More wasn't possible.

EJ: How did the fight for equal rights look from inside? Was the membership of SDS mixed or was it only white?

MS: There were only whites. The Blacks had created their own organization with Stokely Carmichael at the head: the Student Non-Violent Coordinating Committee (SNCC). We called it Snick after the acronym. This was part of a more general development. Martin Luther King's movement included Blacks but also whites, a lot of them Jews of course.

In 1968 and '69, Blacks decided though to act alone. And the movement passed into the Black Power phase. Carmichael was really important in this. He took the African name Kwame Touré. SNCC was the most radical wing of the civil rights movement that said thank you to the whites and goodbye. But, without the whites, it fell apart. At the head of this separatism were the Black Panthers. And the Panthers we really respected.

EJ: Again, all men. There were no women there.

MS: There were a lot. They were everywhere.

EJ: I know, even in the front lines, but always in the rear when it came to decision-making and influence on the course of events.

MS: There were exceptions, but overall, that's the way it was.

EJ: The only well-known name from that company was Valerie Solanas. But Solanas as the one who shot Warhol. And as the friend of Ben Morea, head of the Motherfuckers, who believed that Warhol had murdered art. They both hated Warhol, but she's the one who shot him. She answered for it in court, and she wound up in a psychiatric hospital.

MS: Carl Solomon was also in a psychiatric hospital. That's where he met Ginsberg.[4]

EJ: Yes, but Ginsberg, in distinction from his mother, avoided lobotomy. And this hospital episode in his biography along with a mother with a lobotomy created around him the aura of a *poète maudit*—with all due respect for his poetic work because that is indisputable. And with all due respect for his suffering.

MS: Agreed. But Solanas nevertheless also acted by herself.

EJ: But see how all this looks on the level of cultural representation: even if our ideal of happiness is a little house in the suburbs equipped with

---

4   Ginsberg's seminal poem *Howl* was dedicated to Solomon.

the model of a wife as in Judy Syfers' essay "I Want a Wife,"[5] let's agree that the heroes of this story were Warhol and Morea. Each in his own way. Solanas is remembered as a victim of sexual abuse, a would-be murderess, a manipulated lunatic. Who remembers the literary value of her writings? Her *SCUM Manifesto* is described as a program for the extermination of men, and not as an incisive and phenomenally witty pastiche of patriarchal discourse. Solanas is a kind of freak show threatening the life and health of peaceful citizens: *mirnikh grazhdan Soyedinionnikh Shtatuv Amieriki* [Russian: peaceful citizens of the USA]. And that was supposed to have been this feminine representation.

MS: For us Angela Davis was more important. She was better known. And also Black. I didn't know a lot at the time about Solanas, but it's all pretty important. You'll admit though that elsewhere back then, formal rights and the actual position of women didn't look much better.

EJ: Not only at that time. But in Polish opposition circles Angela Davis didn't seem to enjoy exaggerated respect. In his "Ballad of Highway E7" from 1981, Jan Krzysztof Kelus sang: "That wife of mine is so dainty / Sometimes it's really hard to believe / That she sat longer in prison / Than that lunatic Angela Davis."[6] And do you know what Jacek Kuroń said about revolution? "Because always when there's a revolution, it's the girls who make sandwiches and brew tea …"[7] He stated the fact and simultaneously conceived a reality in which—if you're a woman—you could hardly breathe.

---

5   Feminist essay read by the author in 1970 in San Francisco to an audience assembled to commemorate the fiftieth anniversary of the passage of women's right to vote. The gathering sought to expose the extent of so-called women's work and the *de facto* slave labor of women, pointing to the contradiction between formal equality of the sexes and its actual realization.

6   A singer, composer (and also a professional sociologist) of the anti-communist opposition, Kelus was known as the Polish Woody Guthrie. EJ notes that she was reminded of this text by Henryk Hollender who she would like to thank here for years of generous sharing of his erudition, observations and experiences.

7   Justyna Dąbrowska and Jacek Kuroń, "Dlaczego jestem taki, jaki jestem. Z Jackiem Kuroniem rozmawiała 30 lat temu Justyna Dąbrowska," *Gazeta Wyborcza*, March 8–9, 2014, p. 22. Kuroń was a founder of KOR and later a leader of Solidarity.

MS: I remember one of the seminars at Columbia. Elite. Brandy and cigars. Only guys. It was run by Daniel Bell and Steven Marcus. The Bell-Marcus Seminar. Marcus was the author of an academic cult classic, *The Other Victorians*, about sexuality and pornography in England in the nineteenth century. In another course, he lectured on Shakespeare. His wife, said to be a rather large woman, was named Gertrude. She was also supposedly German. Marcus was Jewish. So, in the context of *Hamlet*, he and Gertrude became the subject of lots of commentary on our part. We would ponder what their sex life was like. We imagined our professor in various roles. But the point of this is that in the final session of the course, on the subject of psychoanalytical interpretations of Hamlet, Marcus announced with holy certainty: "And now the problem of Hamlet is solved." He said this with complete seriousness. It was the heyday of Freud in American academia. We laughed of course, but it was all part of the larger feeling of a community—all male certainly—of the chosen, the elect.

EJ: No surprise that women flipped and decided not to take part any more in their own exclusion.

MS: The second wave of feminism was happening at the same time. And in the same place actually. Several years after me, one of Betty Friedan's sons, Jonathan, studied engineering at Columbia. He lives in Philadelphia now. He's an observant Jew. Years ago, I was at his house for shabbat and there was his mother—an unobtrusive, slightly strange old woman, so unlike her public persona. My oldest son, Zev, was then a little kid, and it was at Jonathan's house that he learned to climb stairs. Today he defines himself as a feminist. He was reading Betty Friedan's *The Feminine Mystique* not long ago. Her grand-daughter, Jonathan's daughter, is an impressive feminist of the next generation.

Chapter 3

Seattle, First Half of the 1970s

EJ: What did you do after the Columbia rebellion?

MS: I had four years of studies behind me and a B.A., then an M.A. in English literature. My thesis, entitled "One Day I Woke Up Dead: The Story of Edgar Allan Poe," received honors. But I didn't feel like doing a doctorate. I gave up the last year of my fellowship. I was even offered an academic position, but I couldn't, I almost physically wasn't able to do it. I walked out on everything and for a year I drove a cab in Manhattan. I drove nights which at that time was pretty risky and looked a bit like Scorsese's film *Taxi Driver*. I drove that same kind of cab, a Checker, which was like a tank. For a while, one cab driver a month was getting killed. At a certain moment, a group of friends and I concluded that we had to leave New York. Some moved to San Francisco and my girlfriend and I moved to Seattle. There, we felt, we could get down to serious activity, serious politics.

My closest friend in Seattle was Bruce Seidel. He was from Chicago. He was a Jew, family from Eastern Europe, traditional, his brother became a rabbi. But his life was revolution. He would say that revolution was the only thing he could do. He was short, five feet four or so, but pretty powerfully built. He rode a Honda 350. He mobilized people. He organized demonstrations. He was involved with a group of prisoners at Monroe Prison who we visited once a week supposedly as part of a program of resocialization. I remember that one of them wore a swastika earring. He didn't know much about the swastika except that it was "bad," that is "cool." We also met a couple of ex-prisoners who had done time for robbing banks in Alaska. With them and some others we started to distribute a newspaper that was written by prisoners, printed outside, then brought by us into the prison.

EJ: What was that paper?

MS: It was called *Sunfighter*. From the Jefferson Airplane song. This was Bruce's idea. "Sunfighter—Gunfighter—/Mount the earth and learn to ride her—".

EJ: Violence, violence, violence.

MS: Sexist objectification. Absolutely. So, this was our first paper. Later, I worked with a man who was a bit older than we were, a black union organizer named Tyree Scott. Charismatic, extremely smart, with a terrific sense of humor. Also a little guy. His organization, United Construction Workers Association (UCWA), fought for the right to work of construction workers who were Black, Mexican, Native American. We picketed the official union, kept after its members. One time we organized a big demonstration, while meantime "someone" quietly destroyed machinery at a construction site. Not me. Here, just as at Columbia, I belonged to a radical group, but I wasn't a leader. I was linked up with people, I was one of them, I wrote for them and in their name, but I moved away when there was fighting. I never held a weapon in my hand. A real intellectual.

EJ: Is that when you did *No Separate Peace*?

MS: Yes. We created the newspaper *No Separate Peace* together: Blacks, Mexicans, Filipinos, Chinese, and Native Americans. The whites were Bruce and me, and Phil Meranto—a young professor at the University of Washington, a terrific guy, who not long after, suddenly died of a heart attack. There were just a few of us, but we were visible. Arriving at a meeting, we'd hear "Oh, the white folks are here." Meaning the ones who put out the newspapers and wrote the leaflets and set all the stuff up using nowadays ancient technology: an exacto knife on a light table.

No Separate Peace, May 15, 1975, vol. 1, nr. 1, p. 1. The paper was published by the United Construction Workers Association from May 1975 to November 1978. Copyright Michael Steinlauf.

EDITORIAL:

Who We Are

This paper will report the news-news about the struggles of Third World, poor, and working women and men to obtain our human rights. The focus will be on news about our communities in Seattle and the Northwest. We will also publish news about those national and international struggles that people locally need to know about in order to see our own struggles in proper perspective.

Our goal is to set up a two-way communications channel into and out of our communities. We want to inform but we need to learn. As the paper begins to develop credibility in our communities, as people begin to trust us, we want people to come to us with news they feel is worth reporting.

The struggle comes first, the paper second.

In the past, many "underground" or "left" papers have fallen into the trap of seeing a newspaper as a primary organizing tool. What often happens is that a group of "independent" people work very hard to produce a paper which is hawked to uncommitted people in an effort to "raise their consciousness." The paper then has a tendency to become, at best, an independent political force, and at worst, a self-serving vehicle for a small group of people who convince themselves they are "doing something."

This paper will be different. Its immediate audience are people who, on some level, can relate to our local struggles and want to know more about them. For example, if someone wants to know about struggles in the Asian community these days, they will find our paper a good source for this information. The purpose of the paper is to take the natural interest and sympathy that already exist around many struggles, and to build increased commitment through a clearer understanding of the issues involved. The struggle defines the paper, not vice-versa.

On the "political line" of the paper --

When a group of people realize that they share a past and present of common oppression, they become a community. When this community begins to deal with its negative self-image, to turn its weaknesses into strength and pride, it develops a culture. When the community begins to act in its own interests, it develops into a movement.

Over the past ten years we have witnessed the flowering of many communities, cultures, and movements:

National groupings -- Black, Chicano, Asian, Native American, Latino;

Sexual groupings -- women, gay people;

as well as workers, young people, soldiers, prisoners, and even neighborhood groupings (Gasside or Beacon Hill or Capitol Hill).

These movements have been a source of strength and pride to their participants. But each of them, as time goes on, develops increasingly severe internal contradictions. The primary contradiction that emerges is between those who will not move beyond their own community and culture, and those who see the need for unity among all oppressed people. We see this contradiction emerging with particular force in all the national movements and in the women's movement.

Many people have gone a certain distance and, for many reasons, have stopped moving. For example -- Black Power and Black Pride and Black Culture developed as a positive force to strengthen and unify the resistance of Black communities to the daily oppression of Black people. But when Black Pride is used as an excuse to ignore the struggles of, say, Chicano people, or when a prominent Black "leader" says about an Asian brother currently involved in the UCWA struggle: "Where was he in '69?" -- this is an excuse for weakness, or an opportunity for racism.

The task of the paper, then, is to encourage all those who want to build principled unity among all the diverse communities in our area, to point out that, ultimately, there is one struggle and one enemy, for there shall be NO SEPARATE PEACE. But building this unity is a very complex process. It won't occur by saying "Black and white unite and fight" like "Open sesame", or by pretending that "After all, we're all workers, ain't we!" The paper will show people that unity doesn't mean sameness -- that being Black or Chicano or a woman can continue to be a source of strength and joy. Therefore, we will emphasize the art and poetry and culture of the various communities in our area, while educating people to struggle against the divisiveness of racism, sexism, and imperialism.

Building unity among our communities means being optimistic about people's capacity for working together, and being optimistic about the future. It means talking about our vision of the future, and explaining how the principled unity we are trying to build will lead to the creation of a humane and just society in which people's real needs can be satisfied.

Where we begin is not where we end. The paper, just like everything else, will go through constant changes. In particular, we have a long way to go in learning to communicate so that people will understand and care about what we say. Fortunately, this is not just our responsibility.

We need constructive criticism from our readers. Tell us what you think of the individual articles, which ones are helpful, which ones make sense, which ones are bullshit.

We also welcome and encourage articles, poems, letters, artwork -- but we can't print everything we receive. Remember that we have a particular point of view, and that point of view is the name of our paper.

Most of all, we welcome and encourage our readers to involve yourselves in the struggles you read about in these pages.

Community Editorial Board	**Staff for this issue**	**Mailing Address**
Douglas Chin	Doug Chin	Suite 1-A
Selma Domingo	Debbie Kaufmann	105 14th Avenue
Larry Gossett	Elaine Ko	Seattle, Wa. 98122
Elaine Ko	Steve Oden	
Raul Salinas	Bruce Seidel	
Beverly Sims	Michael Steinlauf	
	On the road:	
	Robert "Standing Deer" Wilson	

NO SEPARATE PEACE 2

"Who We Are," unsigned editorial by Michael Steinlauf. *No Separate Peace,* May 15, 1975, vol. 1, nr. 1, p. 2. Copyright Michael Steinlauf.

Because Jews were counted as white.[1] So first the whites arrived, then the Blacks, and finally late at night, around midnight or later, the Asians. They'd bring dominos and soon start slapping them down. That was the ritual. A group of Filipino opponents of Marcos were very important. One of them, Selme Domingo, was later killed by Marcos' people in Seattle.

EJ: And the title?

MS: How to say it …

EJ: "Ah, Carl, while you are not safe, I am not safe."[2]

MS: Exactly. No separatism. One for all and all for one.

EJ: Solidarity.

MS: Solidarity. *No Separate Peace* reported on the struggle for equal rights of all groups that were discriminated against, and it generally followed the development of the progressive movement. At a certain moment, though, we became aware that out of those around the *Sunfighter* a small armed group had emerged. Its members believed that public activity, open and legal, was not enough. They believed that the capitalists would never give up, never surrender out of the goodness of their hearts, that the movement had to have an armed wing. At this time, the two ex-prisoners from Alaska became central because they knew how to handle weapons.

EJ: Criminals.

MS: Ex-criminals, yes, but pretty politically conscious. In addition, there were two lesbians, a Black, and several other people. The majority were ex-prisoners. They began to act on their own. And so it started. For example, we're on a march to Oregon, from Seattle to Portland, about

---

1   See Karen Brodkin, *How Jews became white folks and what that says about race in America* (New Brunswick, N.J.: Rutgers University Press, 1998).

2   From Ginsberg's *Howl* (1955); Ginsberg was incarcerated with Solomon at Rockland Psychiatric Hospital.

170 miles, driving part of the way. In Portland we plan on picketing the Bureau of Indian Affairs. It's a march of solidarity with Native Americans and it brought a lot of us together. We overnight somewhere on the road, and in the morning there's reporters all over asking if we know what happened in Portland. We had no idea. It turned out that the Bureau of Indian Affairs had been bombed that night.

EJ: Any killed or wounded?

MS: No. Someone had called in a warning. It wasn't the way it is today. Back then, it was rare for this kind of action to kill anyone. These were exceptional occurrences, accidents, unwanted and unintended. That was also the code that another armed underground group, one that came out of SDS, operated by. It called itself Weatherman after a line in Bob Dylan's "Subterranean Homesick Blues" …

EJ: Music video with Ginsberg!

MS: … where Dylan sings: "You don't need a weatherman to know which way the wind blows." And they also blew up some offices. But our Seattle comrades were an entirely separate crew: the George Jackson Brigade. George Jackson was a member of the Black Panthers. He did time in Soledad, a California prison. His letters from prison were published as a book entitled *Soledad Brother.*

EJ: The introduction was written by Jean Genet, who considered Jackson's death a political murder. So did Foucault for that matter.

MS: George Jackson was shot by prison guards allegedly for trying to escape. A year earlier during an attempt to take hostages—in order to free several Soledad Brothers—Jackson's brother Jonathan, Angela Davis's bodyguard, was killed. It was then that Davis went to prison. Her defense was organized by Bettina Aptheker among others. These were all very well-known things. The George Jackson Brigade was less known somehow, but finally a large monograph came out about them.[3] I didn't

---

3   Daniel Burton-Rose, *Guerilla USA: The George Jackson Brigade and the Anticapitalist Underground of the 1970s* (Berkeley – Los Angeles – London: University of California

know about a lot of the things they did at the time. They placed explosive material into bags of dog food at a Safeway, for instance, as a reprisal for the arrest of Patty Hearst. They phoned the store with a warning, but no one took it seriously and several people were injured.

EJ: What was the connection between *No Separate Peace* and the George Jackson Brigade?

MS: We knew each other. We knew about each other. Bruce was with them. It lasted about two years. The George Jackson Brigade was very active during that time. Until they planned a bank robbery. The bank was surrounded by police. Unclear who had informed. They surrendered, but the police kept firing. Bruce was killed by a bullet in the back. His hands were up in the air. In January 1976.[4] [Long silence.]

EJ: And what did you do then?

MS: Nothing. Nothing. Nothing. The end of the world. [Long silence]. I was living in Bruce's apartment, that is, in the place that he had rented and then passed on to me after he went underground. It was better to disappear from Seattle.[5] An investigation began.

EJ: An investigation in the matter of Bruce's activity or in the matter of his killing by the police?

Press, 2011). And see also Burton-Rose, ed., *Creating a Movement with Teeth: A Documentary History of the George Jackson Brigade* (Oakland: PM Press, 2010).

4   The exact date was Friday, January 23, 1976. Bruce Seidel was twenty-six years old at the time. According to the monograph on the George Jackson Brigade, he died with a gun in his hand. See the reconstruction of the events in Tukwila in Burton-Rose, *Guerilla USA*, pp. 165–70.

5   At news of the events at the bank, "Steinlauf called Michael Withey, an attorney with the Seattle chapter of the National Lawyers Guild who had recently defended a Weather Underground fugitive caught in Seattle. 'I need you to call the Tukwila police and ask if they have a "Peter Wilson" in custody', Bruce's housemate told the young attorney.
      'Who is "Peter Wilson"?' Withey demanded.
      'I can't tell you. He's white, 5'3", with a stocky build and black hair. He's injured.'
      Withey called early the next day. He discovered that 'Wilson' had been admitted into Valley General Hospital, where he was declared dead early that morning. Bruce's housemate, fearing that he knew too much, disappeared. He was aided in his flight by a monetary contribution from what was left of the Brigade" (*Guerilla USA*, p. 169). Not so, according to Steinlauf.

MS: There was never an investigation of Bruce's death. George Jackson Brigade members are either still in prison or—men and women—only recently released. No one was ever found responsible for Bruce's death.[6] [Long silence.]

EJ: Bruce dies.

MS: At this moment, I hear from my mother that her husband has died suddenly. My father died in 1967. My mother married again several years later. Mietek Kwintner was from Piotrków Trybunalski. He'd survived the war in the Soviet Union, I think. He knew five languages, played the violin, loved books. He was a widower with no children. Mom somehow didn't know how to live alone. But this marriage was something else. Several times, despite herself, she hinted at this. Her third marriage lasted about six years.

Bruce Seidel, Seattle, early 1970s. Copyright Michael Steinlauf.

---

6   On February 19, 1976, in a hearing that lasted forty minutes with no questions from the jury, his death was ruled justifiable homicide though forensic evidence showed that he could not have fired his gun (see *Guerilla USA*, pp. 171–73).

Leaflets created and distributed by Michael Steinlauf on the anniversaries of the shooting of Bruce Seidel. In the first leaflet, the poem is Bruce's, in the second the lines are paraphrased from a song *Diana 2*, by Paul Kantner of the Jefferson Airplane.

So I go back for Mietek's funeral and to spend some time with Mom. The day after the funeral, I suddenly get awful stomach pains. At the hospital in Brooklyn, they can't figure out what's wrong with me. After three days in bed, they finally decide it's appendicitis and operate. I'm out after a week, but in the meantime there's a call from Seattle saying it's best for me not to return. Because at first the police thought it was just a normal robbery. But one of them announces: "Do you know who you have? We're the George Jackson Brigade!" A complete cretin. So, then all the investigators went nuts. A real investigation begins—they call a grand jury. If you don't cooperate with them, they have the right to send you to jail for the duration of the proceedings. But I'm not going to snitch on my comrades. I left the hospital, got better. I told Mom what was going on and that I had to disappear for a while, maybe for a couple of months, without leaving an address, that I'd call her from phone booths occasionally. And, in fact, not long after, she was visited by two gentlemen from Washington.

EJ: FBI?

MS: No, not the FBI, the ATF. Bureau of Alcohol, Tobacco and Firearms. They asked, "Have you recently seen your son?" Mom was completely unimpressed. She had survived the war on the Aryan side. So she's like, "Son? What son? Where? What?" She had lightning reflexes and knew how to be tough. But at the end of her life, she was so helpless. She fell, hurt her elbow, and was in a lot of pain. She couldn't sleep. It was a neurological thing. She had several operations, one of which made everything worse. Later, she decided to have a nerve stimulator implanted, but that too gave her no relief, though it was done by some famous professor in Boston. Finally, she spent a month in a pain management clinic where they also tried everything. The director there, a psychiatrist, suggested talking about other possible reasons for her suffering. And here Mom refused: "No, thanks. In that case I'll stay with my pain." I'm no longer sure whether I actually heard that sentence from her, or someone else said it, but she certainly could have said it. One way or another, she refused. She died less than a year later. She didn't live to see my wedding in 1989, or her grandchildren. She wasn't particularly excited about my Jewish studies, but she was relieved. She wanted me to have some stability—education, work, family. She was always worried about me. A real Jewish mother.

But before I left Seattle, something awful happened. I'm at Bruce's house, I'm living there. There's a call and it's Bruce's father. "You all murdered my son," he says. It was terrible. [Whisper.] Terrible. [Long silence.]

EJ: What was your attitude to the use of violence? Did your thinking about it evolve?

MS: Yes. I remember exactly when it was that I understood that you can't do this, can't do it no matter how you rationalize it. It was in the '70s. Groups then that used violence supported each other, even when they had no organizational ties. So that the George Jackson Brigade expressed support for the SLA, that is, the Symbionese Liberation Army, of which Patty Hearst was a member. The Hearsts controlled a significant portion of the American press. The SLA kidnapped her, but then she joined them and robbed banks with them. At that time, when a major hunt for the SLA was in progress, I addressed them directly in an editorial in *No Separate Peace*. "Know where there is shelter," I wrote, meaning that we were there for them, they could count on us to hide them if need be.

Later in the '70s I visited my aunt and uncle in Paris. My aunt died not too long ago, imagine, at the age of 102. At that time in Paris, some terrorist group was placing small charges of explosives in the pockets of jackets that were sold in inexpensive stores. So, working people would reach into the pockets of these jackets and lose their fingers, perhaps their hands, the hands they supported their families with. Our goal had been to smash the rulers, but never to intentionally hurt the people. Now it occurred to me that any kind of turn to violence is part of a continuum. Romantic nineteenth century anarchist bomb throwers to ISIS, where do you draw the line? Nor does the use of violence have any necessary relation to courage. And this, for me, put an end to questions about the use of violence, once and for all.

EJ: There's Jefferson's letter from Paris in 1787. Discussing the project of the American Constitution, Jefferson writes that the Constitution gives the state excessive or unjustified power to assert that its citizens are undermining order. He considered that political freedom would be endangered if citizens—white males, of course—did not retain the spirit of resistance and … access to weapons. He speaks of the periodic need to water the tree of freedom with the blood of patriots and tyrants. And may God protect America, insisted Jefferson, if it didn't stand periodically before just such a citizens' rebellion. In Seattle or earlier at Columbia, when you were the left of the left, were you thinking of change within the limits set by the Constitution, or of overturning the existing order.

MS: No patriotism, no Constitution, zero Jefferson. We were Marxists, internationalists. We wanted revolution and nothing but revolution. We liked Mao. We also liked Fidel. I was even supposed to go on an international work brigade to Cuba, the Venceremos Brigade. Every year a team of intense leftists travelled there to work on sugar cane plantations and build houses. But the George Jackson Brigade and Bruce's death did in those plans. And to answer your question: Jefferson and the Constitution were all part of liberalism for us, and liberalism was something rotten. And don't even mention patriotism. In our opinion—in the days of SDS and also after—this whole setup served exploitation all over the world, and so it was necessary to destroy it completely. I was twenty-six, twenty-seven years old and scary. It's lucky we didn't win. Either I would have been killed or I would have done terrible things fighting the counter-revolution and would probably have been killed anyway at some stage of revolutionary terror. The world demanded change—still does—but not by such methods.

EJ: Was the Holocaust present somehow in the context of your involvement?

MS: On the one hand no. I simply believed that injustice was unacceptable. On the other hand, the Holocaust was always near. Not consciously perhaps, but always present—as a subtext of everything I did. I didn't write "Never again" on a banner. I didn't focus on it in the least, and yet—not counting my escape from home—I didn't try to escape it. This would have been impossible in any case.

In America there's a statute of limitations on being charged for the things I did in the '70s, so I can now talk at length about them. But let me add just one story. Back in the days when Bruce was still with us, before he became part of the armed underground, I had a dog that I went everywhere with. He was a large elkhound with floppy ears. Elkhounds aren't supposed to have floppy ears, so I got him for free. I named him Sasha after the bartender in *Casablanca*. He was an amazing dog. He'd go do his thing, then come back. One time he visited friends for Thanksgiving miles away, returned after three days. One day we're walking around the university campus, Sasha of course, without a leash. We're stopped by university police. Document check, then they call somewhere and find out that just at that time I was supposed to have been at my own trial and that of the other UCW protesters, all of us arrested some weeks before. So they arrest me again. They arrest Sasha. Sasha winds up in an animal shelter. Hearing about this, Bruce on his motorcycle gives the finger to the first cop he sees and winds up in jail too. He didn't want to leave me alone, you understand. Another one of us, a girl named Pilar, was also arrested. After four days in jail, I was brought into court. The judge was a woman. She really wanted to get me out. But as soon as I stood before her, I announced that I didn't recognize the authority of her court because it was an agent of injustice, so she had no choice but to send me back to jail. This was written up in the *Seattle Times*. Nevertheless, without anything more being said, the next day they simply let me out. And Bruce used the occasion to have a special button made up which had the words "Free Michael, free Pilar, hands off Sasha" printed on the outside and "Jobs for all" in the middle. It's my most valued relic of those times. Friends got Sasha out of the pound this time, but later on he wasn't so lucky. Dogs without tags were kept for only three days and then killed, and this was Sasha's fate amidst further confusion. I wept for Sasha as I never have for any human being.

Sasha the puppy with Michael Steinlauf, Seattle, early 1970s. Copyright Michael Steinlauf.

Button by Bruce Seidel. Phot. Elżbieta Janicka.

A 8 **The Seattle Times**   Friday, March 14, 1975

Another job-site protester given jail sentence

By LEE MORIWAKI

Michael Steinlauf, 28, the second United Construction Workers Association demonstrator to stand trial for his role in protest activities at South Seattle construction sites last month, was sentenced to 10 days in jail last evening.

Municipal Judge Barbara Yanick imposed the penalty after Steinlauf said he would not recognize the validity of the court.

Pilar Bueno, the first U. C. W. A. supporter to go on trial, similarly refused to recognize the court system and offered no defense. The 20-year-old University of Washington student from Bolivia drew a 30-day jail sentence from Municipal Judge T. Patrick Corbett on March 6. She was released Wednesday pending an appeal of her case.

NOTING the lighter sentence Judge Yanick gave Steinlauf, U. C. W. A. leader Tyree Scott said, "She's only killing them half dead."

Judge Yanick said Steinlauf, charged with failing to disperse and disorderly conduct, left her no option except to give him a jail term.

Steinlauf, who, according to police, is an unemployed press operator, said he would not pay a fine or court costs, Judge Yanick explained.

Judge Yanick sentenced Steinlauf to 10 days on one charge and suspended a 30-day jail term on the other on the condition he have no further criminal convictions for one year. She said he would not get credit for time he has already served. He was picked up Sunday on a $1,000 bench warrant for failing to show up for an earlier court appearance.

AT ONE POINT in the proceedings, Steinlauf attempted to talk about corporate profits, a key issue in the U. C. W. A.'s campaign for jobs for workers of all races. The judge said those particular remarks were not relevant to the case. Steinlauf replied that he was talking about "justice."

"This is not the forum to talk about justice," Judge Yanick retorted.

Quickly, in response to courtroom laughter, she explained she was not going to turn the courtroom into a place where Steinlauf could "give a lecture on (his) opinions about the legal justice system."

Judge Yanick cleared the courtroom after she was interrupted by members of the gallery as she tried to talk.

IN AN APPARENT switch in courtroom tactics, Ms. Bueno said last night she would appeal her case on the grounds she was the victim of a "political" arrest.

"It's not that I recognize the legitimacy of the courts," she said. "We have to fight for our democratic rights."

Seventeen demonstrators were arrested February 12 and 62 were taken into custody February 13 during protests at the South Seattle job sites around Rainier Avenue S. and Empire Way S.

The U. C. W. A., a minority construction workers' association with about 65 dues-paying members and supporters from many racial groups, including whites, has been fighting for full employment among workers of all races.

Left to right: uncle Marc Wald and aunt Regina Wald (née Zak) visiting from Paris, Doris Steinlauf (née Dwojra Wald, Michael's mother), Michael Steinlauf. California, early 1970s. Copyright Michael Steinlauf.

Chapter 4

Brighton Beach, 1950s

Family c. 1954. Left to right front: Michael Steinlauf, Doris Steinlauf (née Dwojra Wald), cousin Myra Steinlauf (Helen and Eric's daughter), aunt Helen Steinlauf (née Khaya Brokha Wilner). Left to right rear: William (Wolf) Steinlauf, Henry Wilner (Helen's brother), uncle Eric (Arye Yehuda Leyb) Steinlauf (William's brother).

EJ: At the age of sixteen, you escaped from Brighton Beach. What was Brighton Beach?

MS: Today the place is completely unrecognizable. It began to change in the '70s. All the signs are now in Russian. They call it Little Odessa.

EJ: But back then?

MS: The signs were in English and Yiddish. Because there were Jews from Poland there. And elderly local Jews who couldn't afford to move to Florida. Because Brighton Beach is on the ocean, at the very south end of Brooklyn. On one side there's the ocean, on the other the subway which runs on elevated tracks at this point. You can hear waves from one end drowned out every few minutes by the deafening trains. So, who lived there were the Yiddish-speaking old folks and some recent immigrants, so-called refugees, meaning us. Refugees. Awful. I have this friend, similar background, except that his parents lived much longer than mine. And this friend, Mordechai, told me once how at a certain moment in the '90s, his parents and their friends realized that they weren't *refugees* anymore but *survivors.* Can you imagine? Something beautiful! I can see them doing a Polish version of high-fiving each other. But my parents didn't make it to this moment, unfortunately. My father, as I already mentioned, died in 1967, my mother in 1981.

EJ: And that's where you were raised.

MS: Should I now talk about what my parents did before and during the war?

EJ: Well …

MS: They weren't socialists or anything like that, but plain Warsaw bourgeoisie. My mother's father had a clothing and notions store—in Polish it's called *galanteria*—on Nalewki [main street in the Jewish section of Warsaw]. My father and his brother Eric ran a business in hardware and weights.

EJ: What was known as an iron store.

MS: *Ayzngesheft*. At Grzybowski Square of course, because on Grzybowska there were lots of these iron stores and lots of Gerer Hasidim. One of them was a kind of king of iron. He was named Izajasz Prywes. When I was a kid, the name Prywes—one of them seems to have made it to New York—was something to conjure with. My father's family stemmed from Gerer Hasidim—hasidim from the town of Góra Kalwaria, which Jews called Ger because they couldn't live in a town named Calvary Hill—who arrived in Warsaw in the mid-nineteenth century along with their rebbe Alter. My father's brother, who was three years older, was sent to the Gerer rebbe's yeshiva. In fact, he was named Arye Yehuda after the rebbe. And in fact, Arye, that is, Eric, had the temperament of a *yeshive bokher*, a yeshiva boy. But my father rebelled, he didn't want to have anything to do with it. All his life he ran from religion like from fire.

Matseyve [gravestone] of Michael Steinlauf's great-great-grandfather, Gershon Nosn Shtaynloyf, d. January 25, 1881. Jewish cemetery at Okopowa Street, July 31, 2015. Phot. Elżbieta Janicka.

"An honest man […]. He preferred hard work […]. He showed his sons the way to rectitude. His whole life he acted generously and mercifully. Gershon Nosn, son of R. Kalonymus Shtaynloyf, d. on the 25th day of the month of Shvat, 5641. May his soul be bound up in the bond of eternal life."

Top of the *matseyve* of Gershon Nosn Shtaynloyf: bookcase with volumes, designating a man knowledgeable in Torah. Jewish cemetery at Okopowa Street, July 31, 2015. Phot. Elżbieta Janicka.

Matseyve of Michael Steinlauf's great-grandfather, Shmuel Tsvi Shtaynloyf, d. January 15, 1894, son of Gershon Nosn. Jewish cemetery at Okopowa Street, July 31, 2015. Phot. Elżbieta Janicka.

"Place of rest: We are pained by the passing of our dear father, who left this valley of tears [*Emek haBakha*] at the age of 45. Straight and pure was the man buried here, whose name was known and praised by all. His great deeds are praised in all gates, they are his portion in the upper world and will serve him well there. His passing resulted in intense mourning for the family Shtaynloyf, his wife and children who he leaves behind. Here lies the well-known prince Shmuel Tsvi son of R. Gershon Nosn Shtaynloyf of blessed memory, d. on the eighth day of the month of Shvat, 5654. May his soul be bound up in the bond of eternal life."

Matseyve of Michael Steinlauf's great-grandmother, Khaye Soreh Shtaynloyf, d. January 30, 1903. Jewish cemetery on Okopowa Street, January 18, 2016. Phot. Elżbieta Janicka.

"Place of rest and cry of pain: A modest and honest woman. Her whole life her deeds were steered by faith. She showed her sons the path of rectitude. She acted always generously and mercifully. A God-fearing woman Khaye Soreh, daughter of R. Yitshok, wife of R. Shmuel Tsvi Shtaynloyf, d. on the second day of the month of Shvat, 5663. May her soul be bound up in the bond of eternal life."

Matseyve of Michael Steinlauf's grandfather, Moyshe Shtaynloyf, d. March 23, 1930, son of Khaye Soreh and Shmuel Tsvi. Jewish cemetery at Okopowa Street, Warsaw, July 30, 2015. Phot. Elżbieta Janicka.

"Here rests: Bent in homage, your sons stand over your grave as tears run from their eyes. They will weep bitterly and sighs will be drawn from their hearts for you were taken from us in the flower of life. You were a serious and valued merchant. You conducted your trade justly and with an honest heart. All your life you followed the paths of the Lord. You left behind a wife and sons. Moyshe, son of R. Shmuel Tsvi Shtaynloyf, d. on Saturday, the twenty-third day of the month of Adar, 5690, aged 57 years. May his soul be bound up in the bond of eternal life."

Reverse of *matseyve*: "Here rests R. Moyshe son of R. Shmuel Tsvi Shtaynloyf,"
Jewish cemetery at Okopowa Street, Warsaw, July 31, 2015. Phot. Elżbieta Janicka.

Matseyve of Michael Steinlauf's uncle Shmuel Tsvi Shtaynloyf, eldest son of
Moyshe, d. January 23, 1912. Jewish cemetery at Okopowa Street, Warsaw,
July 30, 2015. Phot. Elżbieta Janicka.

"Here rests: For these things I weep; my eye, yea my eye, sheds tears
[Lamentations 1:16] upon the death of my beloved boy Shmuel Tsvi son of
R. Moyshe Shtaynloyf. Died on the second day of the month of Shvat, 5672."
The last two lines of the inscription are inaccessible.

As I was told, there was also a third brother, Shmuel Tsvi, named after the brothers' grandfather, so he was the eldest. I don't know anything about him other than that he died as a kid of appendicitis. My grandfather Moyshe—Moses—my father's father, died in 1930. I was named after him. My father was named Władek, Władysław, Volf in Yiddish, Zev in Hebrew. Moyshe probably inherited this *ayzngesheft* from his father Shmuel Tsvi, and it may be that Shmuel Tsvi inherited it from his father Gershon Nosn, son of Kalonymus. They all lie in the Okopowa cemetery, except for Kalonymus, that is Kalman, but maybe his gravestone was stolen or it's standing there still but undiscovered. After the death of their father, that is, Moyshe, Eric and Władek took over the family business. Eric sat in the store. Władek traveled all over Poland. Typical Jewish business, typical division of labor. There was also an older sister, Runia, who by the time the war began was married with two children.

EJ: How did your father define himself politically?

MS: He belonged to the Zionist youth group Gordonia, but he shrugged off his activity in it, and said he joined because it had pretty girls. He was never in Israel, though the existence of a Jewish state was pretty important to him.

EJ: What kind of education did he have?

MS: He didn't have a university degree. I suspect he completed secondary school with a *matura*, probably a Polish-language Jewish school.

EJ: Maybe a school run by Hitakhdut [Zionist Labor Party], or something similar. Did you think about that?

MS: And from that being a member of Gordonia? Possible. In our family, my mother was the educated one, and my father I considered uncouth though of course he knew not only Polish perfectly, but also Yiddish and Yiddish literature. One time my father couldn't restrain himself and said to me: "You *goyishe kop* [goyish head]—you'll never know who Yitzhak Leybush Peretz was." I always sided with my mother, but that Peretz somehow stuck with me forever, because later I began to read him and study his work which I'm still doing. My father would be proud that I was invited by YIVO[1] to give the keynote lecture for Peretz's 100th *yorzeit*.[2]

EJ: Did your father start a family before the war?

MS: Yes. In the Polish-language monthly *Głos Gminy Żydowskiej* [Voice of the Jewish Community] for 1939, I even found a wedding announcement for Wolf Sztajnlauf and Rywka Rajbenbach.[3]

The religious wedding of Wolf Sztajnlauf and Rywka Rajbenbach was announced in *Głos Gminy Żydowskiej*. In the Polish Jewish daily *Nasz Przegląd* [Our Review] their names appear as Renia and Władysław. The groom also used the Hebrew Zev and the bride the Latin Regina. Behind them a crown probably on the *paroykhes* [Torah curtain] or possibly on the *aron hakoydesh* [Torah ark]. Warsaw, December 1938. Copyright by Michael Steinlauf.

---

1 YIVO - acronym for Yidisher Visnshaftlekher Institut [Jewish Scientific Institute], established in 1925 in Vilna. In 1940, the New York branch became the headquarters of YIVO. "The YIVO quickly became the main scholarly institution of the secular Yiddish cultural movement, and its various publications helped lay the foundation for modern academic work on Yiddish language and literature. It also encouraged work on East European Jewish history" (Ezra Mendelsohn, *The Jews of East Central Europe Between the World Wars* [Bloomington: Indiana University Press, 1983], p. 64).
2 https://www.yivo.org/YL-Peretz-and-the-Forging-of-Modern-Jewish-Culture
3 1939, nr. 2, p. 44, in the list of marriages for December 1938.

EJ: *Nasz Przegląd* didn't publish such information. But at this time a section entitled "For Jewish Refugees" became unexpectedly a shocking social chronicle. In connection with the collection of funds for Zbąszyń,[4] I found this note: "Instead of flowers for the wedding of Miss Renia Rajbenbach and Mr. Władysław Sztajnlauf, from Różka and Lutek Goldminc." Instead of flowers and instead—or rather in the guise—of a blessing for the new path in life. I thought then it might be your father. This information is in the issue of December 13, 1938.[5]

MS: I don't know anything more on this subject.

EJ: And how about your mother?

MS: Before the war, my mother was a young woman, newly married. She had no children. But she had a large family: parents, brother, and two sisters. Her brother left for France before the war, her sisters and their families perished in the ghetto, in Warsaw. They both had children. One, Fela, had an older son, Jurek, the other, Ewa, a young one, Stefcio. Fela's husband fled to the Soviet Union at a time when such things were still possible and when everyone believed that women and children were in no danger. Later, she and Jurek went to Korczak's orphanage. That's all I know about them. They probably died with Korczak during the great deportation.[6]

---

4 Zbąszyń was a town on the western Polish border where 10,000 Jews were held in 1938–39 (another 7,000 were held nearby). In response to Polish laws that threatened to revoke the citizenship of Polish citizens living abroad, Jews with Polish citizenship living in Germany were expelled from Germany but kept by Polish authorities from entering Poland. They were housed in squalid conditions outside the border town of Zbąszyń and their fate became a *cause célèbre* among Polish Jews in the years just before the war. On Novermber 7, 1938, motivated by news of the humanitarian catastrophe in Zbąszyń, the Polish citizen Herszel Grynszpan shot the Nazi diplomat Ernst vom Rath in Paris. This was instrumentalized by the Nazis and used as the pretext for the Nazi-organized series of pogroms in Germany known as Kristallnacht on the night of November 9–10, 1938.

5 "Dla uchodźców żydowskich," p. 9.

6 Henryk Goldszmit, also known as Janusz Korczak (1878–1942), was a physician, writer and educator who, together with Stefania Wilczyńska, maintained an orphanage in the Warsaw Ghetto until he, Wilczyńska, and all the children, along with children and educators from other orphanages in the ghetto, were deported to Treblinka on August 5, 1942, during the great deportation (what the Germans called the *Grossaktion*) of July 22-September 21 when more than 300,00 Jews were murdered.

EJ: That is, presumably not in the ghetto but in Treblinka.

MS: Or somewhere along the way. Summer 1942. You can assume that. About the second sister, Ewa, the one with the younger child, what I assume is that she died together with her child, Stefcio and her husband. But they fought for their lives. They survived the great deportation and built a hideout underground, a bunker. It was apparently a good hiding place. They were well off. They could afford it. They probably put in great efforts. So, they probably died during the uprising. They were shot or gassed or burned. It must have been April or May 1943. In Brighton Beach they talked about their families so often. With names and lots of details. But I had so much of it, I somehow stopped listening, so I remembered little. Friends who come from similar families say the same thing. Though you hear these details hundreds of times, you can't remember them, they don't get into your head. I have all of it written down somewhere.

Jurek, son of Dwojra Wald's sister Fela, late 1930s. Copyright Michael Steinlauf.

Stefcio and his mother Ewa, Dwojra Wald's sister, late 1930s. Copyright Michael Steinlauf.

Shaye Wald and Zisła Wajchenberg Wald, Dwojra's parents, on vacation at the Krynica resort, 1930s. Copyright Michael Steinlauf.

Shaye Wald (1883–1937), Michael Steinlauf's maternal grandfather. Copyright Michael Steinlauf.

My mother was the youngest of the siblings, a cloistered, pampered young lady. Even Warsaw Jews couldn't understand how she could have been raised on Nalewki and never learned a word of Yiddish. She completed a Polish-language Jewish school and then attended the University of Warsaw, where she obtained a master's degree in history in 1933.

EJ: Could your mother as a student of history have had any ties to the Institute of Judaic Studies, that is, Bałaban, Schorr and Schiper,[7] who encouraged their students to study for degrees at Polish universities?

MS: I doubt it. For that you needed to know Jewish languages. And my mother was never interested in Jewish studies. She spoke only Polish, but in her university papers I found her name as Dwojra and not Dorota, which is not exactly evidence of someone aspiring to assimilation. So, diploma in hand, she married a Jewish landowner with property in the

---

7   The Institute was located next to the Tłomackie Synagogue. Majer Bałaban (1877–1942), Mojżesz Schorr (1874–1941), and Ignacy Schiper (1884–1943) were leading Jewish historians. Only Bałaban was granted a university position.

village of Mniszew in Mazowsze in central Poland, not far from Kozienice. His name was Michał Kasman.[8]

EJ: The next Michał in this story. You know, on the cover of the volume *Polskie tematy i konteksty literatury żydowskiej* [Polish themes and contexts in Yiddish literature] there's a map of the regions around Warsaw on which you can see Mniszew. To be exact, it's the automobile map of Polish roads for 1939–40. Inside, there's your essay on Anski's *Dybbuk*.[9]

MS: You know, I didn't notice. But imagine that a photograph survived of two men, the steward and probably Michał Kasman, standing in front of kneeling peasants. During the war, my mother could keep this photograph safely since it wouldn't have occurred to anyone that this feudal gentleman was a Jew. Her whole life she told me that this was one of her friends. Only shortly before her death she admitted that it was her first husband. They married in 1937.

EJ: Your mother's first husband was the owner, the leaseholder, or the administrator of this estate?

MS: I believe he was the owner of the land and a secular Jew. He tried to survive the war on the Aryan side. He had a lot going for him: money, language, knowledge of the Polish surroundings, which he co-created after all. At first, he was supposed to have been shot in some line-up, but the Germans were convinced he wasn't a Jew and they sent him to Pawiak.[10] He sat in Pawiak, then somehow, they let him out. But later he was recognized on a train by some of his peasants. Recognized and turned in. He was gassed at Sobibor. Perhaps he lived to see the uprising which Jewish prisoners organized there in October 1943. Perhaps he participated.

---

8   See "Michael Kasman" in the Central Database of Shoah Victims' Names: http://db.yadvashem.org/names/nameDetails.html?itemId=1164837&language=en

9   See Eugenia Prokop-Janiec and Marek Tuszewicki, eds. (Kraków: Wydawnictwo Uniwersytetu Jagiellońskiego, 2014); the cover was designed by Paweł Sepielak. Anski was the pseudonym of Shloyme Zanvl Rapoport (1863–1920), author of *The Dybbuk: Between Two Worlds*, the most celebrated play in Yiddish theater history. See further.

10 Notorious Nazi prison located within the Warsaw ghetto where primarily Christian Poles were held.

Michał Kasman (1898, Mniszew – 1942[?], Treblinka[?]), first husband of Dwojra Wald. Copyright Michael Steinlauf.

EJ: In the Yad Vashem database it says he was in the Białystok ghetto and that he died at Treblinka, though the Germans were able to send Jews from Białystok equally well to Auschwitz. Born in Mniszew in 1898. His death was reported by his sister.

MS: I don't insist. I'm saying what I remember. My mother certainly told me about his imprisonment in Pawiak. I once travelled to that Mniszew. Little sand dunes. A peasant on a bicycle rides up to me, not young, and asks: "And what's the gentleman doing here?" I tell him I only want to see the place where the manor stood. To which he tells how as a boy he used to deliver eggs and butter "to the palace." I ask him where's that palace. "Sir," he says, "during the war that's where the Ruskies and the Germans fought a tank battle. There's nothing there today."

EJ: The first Belarusian front, the Warka-Magnuszew bridgehead, the battle at Studzianki. I still remember the inscription on the Tomb of the Unknown Soldier because this was the battle route of the First Polish Army.[11]

---

11 The inscription, "Studzianki–Warka 10 VIII–12 IX 1944" was removed from the Tomb of the Unknown Soldier after 1989, that is, after the fall of communism, because it commemorated a Polish but also Soviet victory over the Third Reich.

MS: In the ruins of the servants' building [*czworaki*] I found an iron spike which I took home as a memento, the only thing that remains of that life.

EJ: And what happened with your mother between completing her studies and getting married?

MS: She taught history in some gymnasium, maybe in Warsaw. Or maybe somewhere around Mniszew? Pretty certainly in a private Jewish one because they wouldn't have hired her in a Polish one. And certainly in a Polish-language one, because there wasn't any other possibility. It must have been a school for middle class Jewish children, similar to what she herself had attended. No Yiddish, maybe a little Hebrew. Polish language and Polish culture, though they might have taught a bit about Jewish things, Jewish history or religion, for instance.

EJ: I wanted to ask …

MS: My father had a little boy who was born in 1940 and was killed probably in the ghetto. He had my name. Or rather I have his. He was named Michał, that is, Moyshe. Actually, we were both named after our grandfather. I've got a photograph of Michał and his parents. His not mine. My father never talked about his first family, though he talked about other things quite a lot. I learned about everything in the '70s, five, six, maybe even seven years after his death. After they got out of Poland my parents lived with my mother's brother in Paris. That's where I was born. In the '70s my aunt and uncle were going through their apartment preparing to move to another place and gave my mother a fat envelope "that Władek left." I look, and there are my mother's and my father's *kennkarten* [German identity papers] and lots of other things including evidence of the truth of the improbable stories that my father used to tell. But no trace of my father's first family. I learned a bit from my mother, and more recently, Myra, the daughter of Uncle Eric and Aunt Helen, after Aunt Helen died, gave me photographs of my father and his first wife and the first Michał, taken in the ghetto. [Long silence.]

In the envelope from Paris, I also found proof of a story my father used to tell about breaking his arm when he was hiding on the Aryan side. He was riding in a trolley. It must have been the German section.

Some soldiers started to look at him. So he jumped out of the moving trolley and broke his arm. In that envelope I found a doctor's bill for the cast and the bandage made out to the name on the *kennkarte*.

EJ: Do you know when he got out of the ghetto?

MS: I imagine it was sometime between the great deportation and the uprising. Our relations before his death were so bad that we could hardly talk, so I couldn't ask questions and all I remember is what he had already told on his own. Besides that, he died still as a *refugee*, so no one had done a systematic interview with him. Systematic interviews, as we know, are for *survivors*. I know that he survived the deportation because he had a *shayn*[12]—a pass—and was taken out every day for so-called *shvartsarbet* [heavy labor] on a work squad. He managed to survive this way until the end of September. This was 1942. And later he got out, but I don't know exactly when: October, November, or December. Probably by January, during the renewed deportations and the first battles of the ŻOB [Jewish Fighting Organization] with the Germans, he was no longer in the ghetto. The child was no longer alive. The rest of the family, except for Eric, his wife and daughter, were also no longer alive.

EJ: What about your mother?

MS: When they took her husband to Pawiak, she tried to kill herself. Years later in America in a hospital, one of the doctors, noticing her wrists, asked if she had ever tried to take her own life. She said no. But this wasn't true. She had a momentary breakdown, but you know, what happened at the start of the war was nothing in comparison to what followed. Besides, my mother would say that she survived purely by accident, that she was in no way stronger than anyone else. "Just the opposite," she would say, "I was weaker." A doctor friend, a good person, told her to go from the countryside to his hospital in Warsaw. She spent quite a number of months in this hospital pretending to be sick, I think with a liver ailment. Nuns would visit the patients, so she had to learn the prayers and confession. To the end of her life, when something was going on, she would let out "Jezus! Józef! Maria!"

---

12 Yiddish shortening of the German *passierschein*.

Kennkarte [German identity document] of Stanisława Marianna Langiewicz [Dwojra Wald]. Copyright Michael Steinlauf.

On the whole, she had money. She found some widow who offered to sell her the birth certificate of her deceased daughter. The other daughter, who was later supposedly my mother's sister, was a prostitute, which may have helped divert attention from her. My mother bought the certificate and then had real papers made based on it. My father's *kennkarte* in comparison was amateurish, a forgery obvious to the naked eye.

My mother dyed her hair for the rest of the war, her Aryan looks were not bad, her Polish was impeccable, her manners typical of the intelligentsia. For a certain time, she worked as a servant for a family of the intelligentsia, who had no idea that she was Jewish. It was hard for her, because she had to listen to what this intelligentsia had to say about Jews. When the ghetto was burning, everyone ran out on the roof to look. My mother with them. One says: "Still, I pity the children." To which

Kennkarte [German identity document] of Władysław Michalski [Wolf Sztajnlauf]. Copyright Michael Steinlauf.

another responds: "Watch what you say. Grown Jews would come out of these children someday." And similar stuff. But most often she would talk about that roof. I know my parents' stories only from such snippets, such fragments which I could never put in any kind of order.

Of my father's story, besides the one about the broken arm, I've remembered another piece. About the stove. Also from the Aryan side. They were hiding somewhere inside a large stove or furnace or behind it. Maybe in some nook with an entrance through the furnace? I have no idea. Several people. Someone contacts the Germans and they arrive. The Jews disappear into the furnace. And imagine, one of the Jews lights a cigarette. Nerves. I imagine the others must have put out his cigarette pretty quickly. The Germans didn't notice anything.

EJ: And so in a circle.

MS: And so in a circle. They repeated it all in a circle. Without a break. There's a whole literature on the subject of the silence of Holocaust survivors after the war. I never found anything like that. To cap it all, my mother would invite friends, people just like my parents. They all survived on the Aryan side. They spoke a perfect and completely old-fashioned Polish. For example, they used the expression *nudne jak lukrecja* [cloying as licorice] to mean boring. When I repeated this in Poland, they looked at me as though I'd fallen off the moon. They'd heard it before, but only from people twice my age. Returning to our guests: they came, played cards, old games that no one plays anymore, sixty-six and others. And always told stories. Except for one, who sat by himself on the sofa and usually fell asleep. This was Yasha, the husband of my mother's close friend. He had a number tattooed on his forearm and except for sitting there, took no part in these visits. He didn't say anything, but everything was clear to everyone. The grownups would warn me: "Him you don't ask." But they, one by one, would tirelessly tell their stories from the Aryan side. Certainly in Polish. Everything in Polish. This contact was burned, that hideout was burned, somewhere else I made it, those denounced me, I escaped the others, they shot this one, another time that one, they aimed at me but missed, they chased me but didn't catch me, caught me and I bought my way out. Aryan, Aryan, Aryan, blah blah blah … and about their murdered families. How each died. And that's my childhood, my life in Brighton Beach. I longed for America. And I finally escaped to America. Because Brighton Beach wasn't America.

EJ: Paul Auster recalls this in a recent book, when he writes of your wanderings together in the '60s.

MS: I haven't read it yet. What does he write?

EJ: "We drove to S's [mother's] house in Brighton Beach and then walked down the boardwalk to Coney Island, passing several large clusters of old Jews, huddling in the darkness around 'Old Country' singers. For some reason these quiet spectacles, these doddering old people … speaking nothing but Yiddish and Polish, filled me with a dumb despair, which I tried to ignore by laughing. It was like walking into a dream of one's past, a past seen for the first time, which previously had only been sensed, in the same way that twentieth-century Americans sense what the old frontier was like. [...] The whole night was like that: stepping among corpses, dead things which I had known only from hearsay, now confronted me for the first time in the flesh."[13]

MS: So yes. Though my sense of the boardwalk wasn't death centered.

EJ: Emil Draitser's *Wesele w Brighton Beach* [Wedding in Brighton Beach] describes this from the inside, not naming it.[14] Except that it's already the Brighton Beach of Russian Jews. But how did you imagine the Aryan side, listening to all these stories?

MS: Neither my parents nor their guests, none of them, had anything good to say about Poles. No one. Nothing. Zero. That in the best case, everything was for money, to the last penny. Vicious, merciless. That a German could sooner show some mercy. That Poles were worse than the Germans. And this already I just couldn't accept, because after all it was the Germans who did the Holocaust, not the Poles. I thought about this for years and concluded that whatever else, in this case they exaggerated.

EJ: Władysław Szlengel—before his death in Jakub Kac's bunker at Świętojerska 36—predicted that someday Jews themselves would not be able to believe that the Holocaust happened and looked the way it looked. In his poem "Nowe święto [A new holiday]"—and this new holiday is something like today's Yom HaShoah, he wrote: "The old will praise, / the young will gibe,/ that grandpa worked himself into a fervor./ 'Let the old guy blab,/ it's a bit much for sure/ like with Moses crossing that sea ...'"[15]

MS: I thought that they see it somehow subjectively, but the objective truth is something else. Because that doctor after all helped my mother at the beginning of the war. She couldn't complain. Or her story about *shmaltsovniks* [blackmailers]. She's walking down the street, some *shmaltsovniks* latch on, she gives them some jewelry, something she was

---

13 *Report from the Interior* (New York: Henry Holt, 2013), pp. 257–58.
14 Trans. by Bella Szwarcman-Czarnota (Warsaw: Biblioteka Midrasza, 2008).
15 *Co czytałem umarłym* [What I read to the dead] (Warsaw: Państwowy Instytut Wydawniczy, 1977), p. 91, trans. Michael Steinlauf.

wearing around her neck, and they say they're going to take her to the Germans anyway. But no. They let her go.

EJ: Nice *szmaltsovniks*.

MS: Nice *szmaltsovniks*. That's right.

EJ: Ethical.

MS: It would be worth thinking about how many *shmaltsovniks* took objects and money and then took Jews in to the Germans anyway, and how many only took objects and money.

EJ: Especially that waiting with open arms for Jews who had no objects and money was the army of salvation in the form of the rest of society. Isn't it time to rehabilitate the good *szmaltsovniks*? The bad ones probably too. Without the bad there wouldn't be the good.

MS: It actually makes no sense. It's easy to forget that both my mother and my father came from well-off families, they had enough to buy themselves out until the very end, and they also fought for their lives several months less than others, because they ran from the German-occupied part of Poland in July 1944, as soon as the Red Army crossed the Bug River. For this they would have needed serious money again, and in hard currency.

EJ: And how about your father's family?

MS: Aunt Helen, the wife of my uncle Eric, my father's brother, by some miracle had American citizenship because she had been in the U.S. in the '20s with her parents. Her mother turned up her nose at America—she was a big lady—and her father wasn't able to set up a business, so they returned to Poland. During the war, somewhere near Warsaw there was a camp for such Americans, so she pulled in her husband and daughter, later her brother. Myra—Helen and Eric's daughter—was about five years old at the time. She lives in New York today. Because in January 1944 the Germans loaded these people on a ship to the United States, in exchange for German prisoners-of-war. The story of this camp awaits a monograph.

Helen and Eric Steinlauf with daughter Myra, early 1940s, occupied Poland. Copyright Michael Steinlauf.

EJ: This had nothing to do with the Hotel Polski?

MS: From what I know, no. This is a completely unknown story. And so, my father's brother and his family survived. But a sister and her husband and two children perished, as did my grandmother, whose husband, my grandfather, had died just before the war. I don't know when and how they died, but they were probably taken to Treblinka during the great deportation.

EJ: Where and how did your parents meet?

MS: In Lublin. My father managed to get to Lublin as soon as the Red Army got there. So that, as I've said, he fought for his life several months less than others. The same for my mother, who also immediately headed for Lublin. This saved them, although, as we know, dangers didn't end with the arrival of the Red Army. They didn't even end with the war, but despite everything, this was already a different life. In August in Lublin the first group of Jewish survivors, some three hundred, met and elected a chairman, a vice-chairman, and a recording secretary. My father was the recording secretary. He filled this function from August until October. I know this because the minutes, written in his hand, survived and my friend Professor Monika Adamczyk-Garbowska made me copies of them. They had been the subject of a master's thesis written by one of her students.[16]

---

16 Adam Kopciowski, *Żydzi w Lublinie 1944–1949* (unpublished master's thesis, Department of Contemporary History, Maria Curie-Skłodowska University, Lublin, 1998). The advisor was Zygmunt Mańkowski.

EJ: This was under the auspices of the Central Committee of Polish Jews [Centralny Komitet Żydów Polskich, CKŻP]?[17]

MS: No, it was earlier. This was the germ of the CKŻP. It was called the Jewish Aid Committee [Komitet Pomocy Żydom] and it was formed in Lublin on August 10, 1944.

EJ: And what is the founding family myth?

MS: It goes like this. My mother came to the Jewish committee looking for a place to stay. My father oversaw such things. He referred her to a certain address which, however, no longer existed because the building didn't exist anymore. So, she returned, and this time, as my father would say, "I didn't let her go." That's how my story begins. My father had good relations with the mayor of Lublin, and he told him the way things were: "You're a Jew, an official of a Jewish organization, sooner or later you'll get a bullet in the head."

EJ: Both your parents must have been in Lublin when Leon Feldhendler, one of the few survivors of Sobibor, was shot. He was a subtenant, by the way, in a room in a building near the marketplace that belonged to the Arnsztajns before the war, the family of whose members you'd later write about. That's where Franciszka Arnsztajnowa, poet, subtenant of Polish culture, lived. Even in the context of the postwar violence directed at Jews, the murder of Feldhendler, who was one of the leaders of the uprising in Sobibor, must have made an impression.[18]

---

17 The Central Committee of Polish Jews served the needs of Jews in Poland after the war. It functioned from the fall of 1944 to 1950.

18 EJ adds the following from the postwar testimony of Feldhendler's wife: "On April 2, before seven in the evening, we were sitting in our room. It was the last room, we were subtenants. I heard movement in the landlord's room. I was lying on the couch, reading a book. He was writing something. I had a bad feeling, but all I said was 'Leon, it's them.' He went up to the door, took hold of the doorknob. There was a shot. One shot through the door" (cited according to Hanna Krall, "Wyjątkowo długa linia," in *Wyjątkowo długa linia. Spokojne niedzielne popołudnie* [Warsaw: Świat Książki, 2010], p. 87). On October 14, 2018, the family of Leon Feldhendler was awarded the Commanders Cross of the Polonia Restituta Order on behalf of Polish president Duda, an emblematic example of the cynicism of the current authoritarian right wing Polish regime known for its antisemitic historical politics.

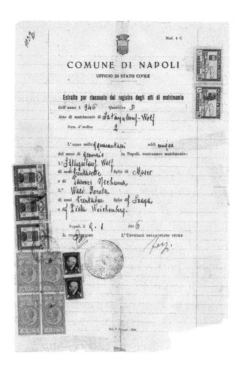

Marriage certificate of Wolf Sztaynlauf and Dorota Wald, Naples, January 5, 1946. Copyright Michael Steinlauf.

Refugees: Wolf Sztaynlauf and Dorota Wald, Italy, c. 1946. Copyright Michael Steinlauf.

MS: I didn't know about Feldhendler. In any case, my parents didn't wait for the Kielce pogrom, and after several months in Lublin left Poland. With no papers. Just with money. Finally, through Hungary among other places, they reached the camp at Santa Maria di Leuca in Italy. I just got information about this camp on the internet page of the Holocaust Museum in Washington. They were there for quite a few months. They got married in Naples. I have their original marriage documents. I also have a manuscript of my father's about the ghetto. Fifteen pages on closely written legal-sized pages in Polish.

EJ: What happened next with your parents?

MS: They were in the UNRRA [United Nations Relief and Rehabilitation Administration] refugee camp at Santa Maria di Leuca when they found out that my mother's brother and his wife were alive and still living in Paris. Majer Wald and Regina née Zak, a very fine aunt, a real Litvak from a wealthy Moscow family. They didn't go to the Vél d'Hiv,[19] and later hid under false papers. My aunt later told me about various of her adventures, adding that it was all like nothing compared to what my parents went through. My parents decided to get through to them. Illegally of course. A specially trained female guide from UNRRA took them across the Alps in spring. You couldn't get caught illegally crossing the border because then they would send you back. But once you were in France, no one bothered about your papers. On the way—and this is another piece of my origin myth—my mother looked down into some chasm, got hysterical, my father socked her, and she calmed down. Probably true.

My parents find my uncle and aunt in Paris. My father doesn't want much more to do with Europe and would rather live closer to his brother in New York. My mother would prefer to remain in Paris. Finally, they apply for an American visa for which they wait for four years. I'm born after a year.[20] We leave for America when I'm three years old. In 1950.

---

19 The roundup of the Vél d'Hiv on July 16–17, 1942, was the largest mass arrest of Jews in occupied France. Over thirteen thousand Jews, including four thousand children, were taken by French police and held for five days at the Vélodrome d'Hiver, an indoor bicycle track and stadium, after which they were shipped to transit camps and from there to Auschwitz.

20 Michael Steinlauf was born on February 19, 1947.

Three-month-old Michael Steinlauf with his mother, Brunoy, France, May 30, 1947. Copyright Michael Steinlauf.

EJ: You speak French and you're a Frenchman.

MS: I still speak French without much of an accent, though in general of course I replaced French with English.

EJ: You reached Brighton Beach.

MS: Not right away. After about a year.

EJ: And there you came to know the problematic of the Holocaust with particular reference to the Warsaw ghetto and the Aryan side.

Wolf, Dorka and Mishelek, France, 1947. Copyright Michael Steinlauf.

MS: That's what I was raised in. But although from the cradle I heard about the Aryan side, there was not something like the Holocaust. There was the war. A single Polish word: *wojna* [pronounced voyna]. This *wojna* was the subject of stories which I listened to endlessly. The first time in my life I heard the word "Holocaust," I was around eighteen years old, at Columbia. And it was as if lightning struck me, because I suddenly understood that "Holocaust" was what my parents called *wojna*. And so, I jumped with both feet into the macrohistory, which of course I've never left, because it was my history from the beginning, sometimes too much so. I felt at home but also strange.

EJ: Meaning?

MS: Something so intimate, so very private like our war, suddenly became accessible to everyone, public. Before I kind of thought that it was just our thing, about our family, neighbors, friends. Some kind of weirdness, because I saw that outside Brighton Beach and generally in America, people didn't live this way. For example, I saw they had extended families. In Brighton Beach people didn't have relatives, they functioned singly or in couples. The couples were either childless, or they had one child born after the war. You'd frequently see not-so-young parents with a little child. Among these children I was a total rarity because I was the only one who spoke, not just understood, Polish. My parents claimed they'd encouraged this for me to be able to communicate with my aunt and uncle in Paris.

There's an early moment of transition, Poland to America, that rooted itself in my memory. I must have been about five years old. My father came home from the barbershop with his mustache shaved off. It totally didn't look like him and I started crying. It took him a while to convince me it was him.

Another time in Manhattan, when I was older, we lived through a moment of danger. Thirty-fourth Street. We're walking out of a department store, talking about something, when suddenly some guy calls after us in Polish: "*Rodacy* [Countrymen]!" My mother freezes. And my father: "I'll give him *Rodacy*!" And they shot down the street away from this *rodak* as fast as they could. For a long time, they didn't quiet down. My father would repeat, extremely upset, "I'll give him *Rodacy*!"

And so, when I got that Fulbright to travel to Poland, I didn't know how to tell my mother. I was afraid. My father wasn't alive any longer. I didn't know how to start talking to her about it, and in addition she was not well, and I didn't want to leave her. And finally, I never did tell her, because imagine, she died. A good Jewish woman. A good Jewish mother. She died to not make a big deal out of herself. It was a shock. In December 1981, martial law was declared in Poland, and soon after I get a phone call from Florida, where my mother used to spend the winter. Some policeman calls: "Your mom is dead." Something awful. I flew to Florida, arranged to bring my mother back, the funeral was in New York. [Silence.] And so, I could go to Poland, though I had to wait until the political situation cleared up a little. I arrived in March 1983, a few months before the suspension of martial law in July. Later, in the '90s, some of my parents' friends decided to travel to Poland. Knowing my parents, I doubt they would have decided to go. But who knows?

So, returning to the beginning, I fled Brighton Beach at the age of sixteen when I received a four-year scholarship to study at Columbia. My parents remained of course where they were, and for the first year I returned to them every weekend. Later it changed. I distanced myself from them. And it seemed to me that I'd freed myself from it all.

Chapter 5

Brandeis, 1979–88

EJ: When did you become interested in what you call Jewish things?

MS: Only after Seattle.

EJ: How and why?

MS: After Bruce's death, my mother's husband's funeral, my operation and so on, I hid for half a year. Finally, though, I had to do something, and I had friends near Boston. That's where all the universities are, Harvard, Brandeis, and the rest. Thinking about the years I spent in Seattle, I came gradually to the conclusion that the most important thing for me was not leftist politics, but national identity. In *No Separate Peace* each group was rooted in its own culture: Black culture, Chinese culture, Chicano culture. They had their own codes, understood each other within them, laughed at the same jokes. For instance, those who identified as Chicanos were able to use their legendary land of origin, Aztlán (today northern Mexico and southwestern United States) in an ironic way. I would hear one say to another: "I come from Azt-lán, man." To which the other replies: "Yeah, I come from a-slum too." This, it struck me, was exactly like the irony in Sholem Aleichem, who on one page references King Solomon and the Temple and on the next page a muddy, impoverished shtetl in Eastern Europe. But I supposedly didn't have my own Aztlán. It occurred to me that maybe my Aztlán was the world of my parents—the one that was irretrievably gone.

I signed up for an evening Yiddish course in Boston taught by Hinda Gutoff who, as it turned out, had survived the Warsaw ghetto as a child. Later I applied to Brandeis. There I met Joshua Rothenberg, a Jew from Radom who survived in the Soviet Union, and later became the Judaica librarian at Brandeis. Officially he was the Judaica librarian, but they also had him teach Yiddish and Eastern European Jewish history. He'd studied in a Jewish gymnasium in prewar Radom, and he knew an amazing amount, not just books but more, what in Yiddish is called *lebnshteyger*—customs, lifeways. I studied under him and wrote my doctorate under him, though officially it was someone else because Rothenberg didn't have a doctorate. I was thirty-one years old when I got to Brandeis and in contrast to most of my fellow students, I knew exactly what I was looking for. I wanted to learn about the world of my parents.

EJ: Though Yiddish and shtetl was not the world of your parents.

MS: My *mameloshn*,[1] my mother tongue, is Polish. And Yiddish was not what I heard at home, agreed. But this was the original language of Eastern European Jews. Specifically, I was interested in the world of Polish Jews in the interwar period.

EJ: Which was extremely varied …

MS: One way or another, I had to learn Yiddish. When you're studying academically, you have to study everything. Rothenberg assigned me a Yiddish novel to read every couple of weeks, and we would discuss the novel's language but also the beliefs and customs that were referenced in it, that is, we'd look at it from an ethnographic point of view. Rothenberg wasn't interested in theories, but in facts, that is, how Jews actually lived. I learned a vast amount from him.

EJ: What did you write your doctorate about?

---

1   The Yiddish word means "mother tongue" but also imbedded in it is the strong historical connection to women, that is, "mother's tongue." And characteristically for Yiddish, the word is made up of a European component (*mame*) and a Hebrew one (*loshn* or *lashon* in modern Hebrew).

MS: I was looking for a figure linked simultaneously to both Yiddish and Polish cultures. This was hard, because in the interwar period there were very few such people. Many Jews knew Polish perfectly, many were active in Polish culture, but being creative in both cultures was rare. I discovered Mark Arnshteyn, who in Polish took the name Andrzej Marek.[2] Arnshteyn was suggested to me by the great Israeli scholar of Yiddish culture, Chone Shmeruk, who was then at Brandeis for several months. Later on, I visited him in Israel. We concluded that in comparison to the vast amount of material required to study other figures, Arnshteyn was doable. And also fascinating. In Israel I also received bibliographical pointers from Shmeruk on the work of the great Yiddish writer, Y. L. Peretz, who I've been writing about for years.

EJ: Was Arnshteyn related to the doctors Arnsztajn and Franciszka Arnsztajnowa from Lublin?

MS: It's the same family. Franciszka was related to the Arnshteyns by marriage. Arnshteyn was born at the end of the 1870s. His first work— or one of them—was entitled *Der vilner balebesl* [The little Vilna householder] and was about a semi-legendary Vilna cantor who attempted a career on the Warsaw opera stage. He was known as *der vilner balebesl* because of his marriage at age thirteen to the daughter of the wealthiest merchant in Vilna. The name is both ironic and endearing.

EJ: The one associated with Moniuszko?[3]

MS: That's the one.

---

2   On Mark Arnshteyn see Michael Steinlauf, "Mark Arnshteyn and Polish-Jewish Theater," in Yisrael Gutman, Ezra Mendelsohn, Jehuda Reinharz and Chone Shmeruk, eds., *The Jews of Poland Between Two World Wars* (Hanover, N.H.: University Press of New England, 1989), pp. 399–411. See also Michael Steinlauf, *Polish-Jewish Theater: The Case of Mark Arnshteyn; A Study of the Interplay among Yiddish, Polish and Polish-Language Jewish Culture in the Modern Period*, unpublished doctoral dissertation, Department of Near Eastern and Judaic Studies, Brandeis University, 1988.
3   Stanisław Moniuszko (1819–72), Polish opera composer whose works, cornerstones of the Polish national canon, celebrate the cultures of both Polish peasants and nobility.

EJ: Joel-Dawid Lewensztajn-Straszuński. Buried in the Okopowa cemetery, by the way. He started to make a career in opera and didn't end well. Considered a servile singer of tunes, what both Jews and Poles called *mayufes,* symbol of Jewish toadying before the Christian majority in a situation in which the other side lacks all respect for Jews.[4] I saw a film about him, a musical. Totally over the top. Moniuszko there is a fine Polish gentleman, master of art and style, in a fur coat down to his ankles, top hat, and mustache. The complete negation of Moniuszko.

MS: Arnshteyn's play was not quite so over the top. But you're talking about the American Yiddish film *Overture to Glory.*[5]

EJ: An American Yiddish film with English subtitles. It begins on Rosh Hashana, ends on the eve of Yom Kippur, the soundtrack is synagogue choirs. Straszuński—clean-shaven and dressed Polish folklore style— bows to the Christian public in a Polish salon. "I kiss your sweet hands and fall to your little feet." A hat with a feather. Hardcore.

MS: This was probably supposed to be the aria sung by Jontek, the devastated lover from Moniuszko's opera *Halka.* This was one of the last Yiddish films in general. In America, they made a film with a happy ending out of this. *The Jazz Singer,* starring Al Jolson, was the first sound film. There were lots of other adaptations.

EJ: This I don't know. But maybe what I saw was supposed to have a "happy ending." The hero, who's lost his voice, regains it after numerous wanderings and returns to his synagogue to sing. *Kol nidre* of course.[6] He sings so beautifully that the community forgives him. Up in the women's section, even the wife he abandoned forgives him. And, amid all this general forgiveness, he falls dead.

---

4   The expression *zingen mayufes,* meaning to entertain, or by extension, to behave, in a fawning, cringing way before one's Polish "betters," is found in both the prewar Yiddish and Polish lexicons. See Chone Shmeruk, "*Mayufes*: A Window on Polish-Jewish Relations," *Polin* 10 (1997): 273–86.

5   Max Nosseck, *Overture to Glory / Der Vilner Shtot Khazn* (1940).

6   Aramaic text declaring a release from religious vows and obligations that were made unintentionally or under duress. It is recited in synagogues at the opening of Yom Kippur eve services.

MS: Which couldn't happen by the American standards of the happy ending. *The Jazz Singer* is fully optimistic. It's a truly American version, without Yiddish, without the abandoned wife, without God's punishment. Without tragedy. Entirely different from Arnshteyn's. Arnshteyn first wrote the play in Polish, only later in Yiddish, and then *Der vilner balebesl* had quite a career, popular on both sides of the Atlantic. The original Polish version written at the turn of the century was called *Pieśniarze* [Singers]. On the heels of his success, Arnshteyn left for America. He spent years on the east and west coasts, as well as in South America. In 1924, he returned to Poland and began to translate and stage the classics of the Yiddish theater in Polish. For example, he translated *The Dybbuk*, which in Poland today is known in the translation of Michał Friedman. He also translated H. Leyvik's *Golem* as well as Jacob Gordin's perennially popular *Mirele Efros*. The play is structurally similar to *King Lear*, but without the tragedy. Mirele Efros has three sons. She is a proud and tough-minded businesswoman, a widow who's taken over her husband's business. But the "Jewish Queen Lear" is pushed out by a brutal daughter-in-law. Various intrigues follow, but everyone finally reconciles on the occasion of the bar mitzvah of Mirele's grandson.

EJ: Wait, as I've seen on a film poster on the internet, it was Arnshteyn who directed this in Poland in 1912: "Story of a Proud and Venerable Widow, Who Sacrifices All for the Love of Her Children, and They Don't Repay Her Very Well. In the main role the celebrated theater artist Ester-Rokhl Kaminska. With family. Directed by Andrzej Marek."[7] This was the screen debut of Ida Kaminska.[8] A Yiddish film hit.

MS: But that was before the First World War. Golden days for Yiddish theater. In the 1920s, at a certain moment Arnshteyn was attacked by yiddishists who accused him of encouraging Jews to give up Yiddish for Polish.[9] But those Yiddish plays he staged in Polish were popular among

---

7   *Mirele Efros*, n. d. See Władysław Banaszkiewicz and Witold Witczak, *Historia filmu polskiego*, v. 1 (Warsaw: Wydawnictwa Artystyczne i Filmowe, 1966), p. 65.

8   Ester-Rokhl Kaminska (1870–1926) and her daughter Ida (1899–1980) were central figures in the development of Yiddish theater for nearly a century. See further.

9   Nevertheless, it seems clear that linguistic—though not national—assimilation was the future of the Jews in Poland. Ezra Mendelsohn sums up the linguistic—and

Jews and brought Jewish culture to Jews who needed it because they had already lost Yiddish. In the Polish world, his mission was hardly noticed. Jewish plays didn't concern Poles even a little, though he translated them into Polish with a Polish audience in mind. True, Zelwerowicz, Boy-Żeleński[10] and some others were fans of his. Boy reviewed his Polish versions of Yiddish classics. It was Boy who described *Mirele Efros* as the Jewish *King Lear*, and acclaimed Arnshteyn's staging with Wanda Siemaszkowa in the title role. He praised Arnshteyn himself: "He translates the works himself, renews them, stages them. [...] He dreams of creating a theater 'on the border,' as it were, bringing the Jewish masses to Polish theater, and interesting us in Yiddish theater, to mutual advantage."[11]

EJ: So, I go with Shmeruk—that's indeed my role in our performance: "Alongside fascination with the unknown, this 'exotic' interest became the typical reaction of Polish critics to Yiddish literature. We do not have to analyze Polish critical works any more closely [...] in order to establish their leading characteristics. We see them clearly in the reviews of Tadeusz Boy-Żeleński, a generous and open lover of Yiddish theater. [...] Żeleński, noting the elements touching Polish literature, closes his comments by repeating, though in a new way, those same random impressions on the subject of Yiddish literature that Polish critics had repeated to boredom for decades: 'And one thing struck me. Does it make any sense, living beside each other, to not know each other so completely? We put on plays from all over the world, often trivial and lame, but we do absolutely nothing to get to know the soul of a nation with whom we're destined to live together.' The foreign 'exotic' character and the distance

the larger cultural-political—evidence as follows: "It is safe to assume that, had independent Poland survived for another twenty years, modern Yiddish and Hebrew culture and schools would have inevitably declined, to be replaced by Jewish cultural creativity in the Polish language" (*The Jews of East Central Europe Between the World Wars*). In this respect, Arnshteyn was a pioneering figure. And see Eugenia Prokop-Janiec, *Polish Jewish Literature in the Interwar Period* (Syracuse, N.Y.: Syracuse University Press, 2003).

10 Aleksander Zelwerowicz (1877–1955) was an actor, director, and teacher. Tadeusz Boy-Żeleński (1874–1941) was a writer, translator, and theater critic.

11 Tadeusz Boy-Żeleński, "Flirt z Melpomeną. Wieczór siódmy i ósmy," in his *Pisma*, v. 22 (Warsaw: PIW, 1964), p. 485.

of a literature, which from time to time is 'discovered,' supported the illusion that a Chinese wall separated it from Polish literature. But the physical distance between the two literatures was no greater than that between Krakowskie Przedmieście and the Yiddish theater on Oboźna Street. [...] This distance was rarely conquered and crossing it did not bring desirable results."[12] But you yourself have written that Poles—the well-wishing ones—often wrote about Jewish society as "an exotic 'dark continent' lying behind a 'Chinese wall.'"[13]

MS: The Polish audience indeed didn't go to see his plays.

EJ: The story of Arnshteyn has something in it of the story of Straszuński.

MS: Of course. It's the same story. It was all pretty bitter. *Der vilner bale-besl* turned out to be Arnshteyn's greatest success and at the same time his curse, because of all his original works, most Jews didn't want to see anything else. Arnshteyn's career began with this work and ended with it, staged by the Nowy Teatr Kameralny [New Chamber Theater] that he had established in the Warsaw ghetto. *Pieśniarze* was immensely popular in the ghetto. *Gazeta Żydowska*, the official newspaper of the ghetto, wrote on January 16, 1942: "Grand festive premiere today on Friday at 5:45. Directed by the author. Hall well-heated and lit."[14]

EJ: Let's add that, behind the walls, there were five Jewish theaters of which two performed in Polish. And Nowy Teatr Kameralny was the largest of these. It was located on the grounds of the Church of St. Augustine. In well-known postwar photographs, amidst the rubble of the ghetto, only this church remains standing. We don't know whether productions were staged in the cellar of the church or in the parish house, but the theater was definitely installed there. Its activity was inaugurated with the staging of *Mirełe Efros*—under the Polish title *Mirla Efros*—directed by

---

12 Chone Shmeruk, *Legenda o Esterce w literaturze jidysz i polskiej. Studium z dziedziny wzajemnych stosunków dwóch kultur i tradycji* (Warsaw: Oficyna Naukowa, 2000), pp. 107–09.

13 *Bondage to the Dead*, p. 19.

14 See Ruta Sakowska-Pups, "O działalności teatralnej w getcie warszawskim," *Biuletyn Żydowskiego Instytutu Historycznego* (Warsaw), nr. 69 (1969).

Arnshteyn who functioned in the ghetto definitively as Andrzej Marek. During the year of his theater's existence, the play was performed seventy-six times. Record popularity. The star of the production and of the theater in general was Michał Znicz.[15]

MS: Znicz managed to stay alive almost to the end of 1943. He perished on the Aryan side on Christmas Eve. Arnshteyn also probably lived through the Jewish uprising. He was either murdered at Treblinka or shot in the ruins of the ghetto.

EJ: All this makes me want to back up, to ask you more about the beginning and about your transition into Jewishness.

MS: Fire away.

EJ: How was it that you first felt a relative lack of identity and community in Seattle in the first half of the '70s while acting in the name of social justice and general emancipation?

MS: Regardless of our common goal, each of us—assembled around *No Separate Peace*—belonged to some national group. And I? I was a Jew, but who did I belong to really? Not to "American Jewry," which I wanted to have nothing to do with, which I found disgusting. So, who was I? A Jew, one of two who wrote leaflets in the name of everyone, the whole collective. I had no national group behind me to relate to, and I felt that it wasn't good to be nothing more than an isolated, individual being. And out of this came my national engagement.

EJ: And you couldn't be a Jew just as you were? Like Ginsberg, Auster, Marcus, Bell—many others, because not just those few who were linked to Columbia.

MS: Like Norman Mailer? Like Bob Dylan? No, that wasn't enough for me.

---

15 Michał Znicz (1884–1943) was an acclaimed Polish actor. He was of Jewish origin and was locked in the Warsaw ghetto.

EJ: What did you lack?

MS: Brothers. Brothers and sisters. Brotherhood and sisterhood were a creation of internationalism, it's true. Internationalism was the project of rooting yourself in humankind, in humanity. And this was a brilliant idea! But I lacked roots, I would say, of an intermediate kind. In general, people in the nineteenth century—not to mention today—lacked this, they needed something in between, and nation turned out to be the answer. I've thought a lot about this, what it means to be a Jew. At Columbia, I had a young professor who once told me: "You can't be a socialist by yourself. You need others for this, a group, a party." I changed it a bit, telling myself: "You can't be a Jew by yourself."

EJ: And you'll say this to people who *are* Jews by themselves?

MS: But is Jewishness for them important in any way? It seems to me that a purely individual identity is a Christian idea. But to be a Jew something else is important. When I go to my synagogue on Yom Kippur and wrap myself in my talles, I isolate myself from others but at the same time I hear their voices. I'm a part of a group that's praying. I haven't done this in a while, but it's a good example. To be a Jew means to be connected to other Jews. You then have the feeling of belonging to the group, but also a responsibility in relation to the group. Not against others, not in relation to others even. It's not that I respect others less. I continue to feel solidarity with others, and I respect others—just like in the years of *No Separate Peace*. The concept of nation is convoluted and tangled. Like the feeling of belonging. I know how easy it is to fetishize one's own group, yet I still think that such groups are important.

EJ: To whom?

MS: Not just to me. To others too.

EJ: But not everyone.

MS: Not everyone, but many.

EJ: Loyalty so defined can easily turn into subordination, don't you think? How about individual agency? How about individual responsibility? Wouldn't it be safer ethically to identify with people who share your values, for in this area—notice—divisions run across groups?

MS: Certainly. I don't identify with Israel, for example, and I don't think of taking responsibility for Israel. But what happens there awfully bothers me. More than what happens elsewhere.

EJ: In this case, you're not an exception because most Europeans are awfully bothered by what happens in Israel, in contrast to what happens elsewhere. India occupies Kashmir, Morocco does what it wants in occupied Northern Sahara, various despots run amok the length and breadth of the world, blood flows, in the '90s we had a horrible war in Europe. No problem. Seventy-five percent of the resolutions of censure issued by the U.N. Security Council are aimed at Israel. People are awfully bothered by what happens in Israel, though at the same time no one thinks to take responsibility for Israel.

MS: That's interesting. I know why I care so much about what Israel is up to, but why does it also concern Europeans so much? I may have forgotten how that word sounds. Isn't it "antisemitism"? But let's return to nationalism. Maybe I'll say it differently. What I'm after is difference that's not tied to value judgment. My group isn't better. Other groups aren't worse. It's so important to keep to this. It's not easy, but I believe that attachment to one's own group doesn't condemn us to chauvinism.

EJ: You've said what one gains. But what does one lose in such an identity regime?

MS: One stops being an internationalist. But I'm not sure I lost a lot with this. Maybe I lost something that can't be attained in any case? I had friends, I had comrades in the struggle, but that didn't do it. I guess I felt very alone. I needed some closer, narrower community. My friends, my comrades in struggle had this. I didn't.

EJ: Their belonging to a given group was primary. They brought it with them, whether they wanted to or not. They didn't have to construct it. Just the opposite, they wanted to deconstruct it.

MS: Even they had to construct a lot. Increasingly nowadays, construction—and deconstruction—of identity is a fact of people's lives. Take Malcolm X, who went through several shifts of identity, came to Islam, and then evolved further within it. But without a doubt, the common denominator of all these quests was the dream of changing both the world and relations within one's own group. That's the sort of group I wanted to have. And I chose the Jewish nation.

EJ: But one can be in the Jewish nation in many ways, and we know that supporters of various options would often not even shake hands.

MS: Truly! Israel makes me crazy. So, I'd say about myself that I'm a diaspora nationalist. That, I decided, is how to best define my nation.

EJ: Which nation concretely?

MS: First of all, Jews in communities all over the world. I feel an affinity with them that I'd call national. Beyond that, though, the nation that's gone. The nation that vanished so completely, so irretrievably. I feel part and parcel of it. And within that nation, secular Yiddish culture in particular.

EJ: Before the war, Yiddish was used by some eleven to thirteen million people with very different Jewish identities in Eastern Europe and the United States. Today there are at most six hundred thousand people all very similar to one another—*haredim*, that is, Orthodox Jews—whether in America or in Israel or in London or Amsterdam or Paris. Only they use Yiddish as their daily language. As the yiddishist Agata Kondrat writes: "Their Yiddish, however, does not resemble the language heard on the streets of prewar Warsaw or Vilnius. Under the influence of local languages, it underwent many changes, sometimes lost its characteristic resonance, but enriched itself by borrowing from other languages or sometimes even took over foreign grammatical structures."[16] From the point of view of yiddishism, that is, the secular Yiddish ethos, which gave birth to the culture you love, including YIVO, it's the end of the world. But returning to the main point: this wasn't a choice that imposed itself on you. Your family's resources offered other possibilities.

MS: Certainly, I had other options closer to hand: Polish intelligentsia from my mother, the line of Ger—lapsed, to be sure—from my father. But I became fascinated with Yiddish and the world of modern Yiddish culture. A world away from Israel and a negation of American Jewry, all those Americans of Jewish descent. But maybe from my father after all. He knew Yiddish well and loved Peretz...

EJ: Could you characterize what you call "American Jewry," "all those Americans of Jewish descent"?

MS: It's hard to give a simple answer because it's a complex phenomenon. But as a start I'd distinguish two main groups. On the one hand, those who belong to a Jewish organization: synagogues, Jewish federations, "Jewish centers," those who send their kids to Jewish summer camps. For them, to be a Jew is to be like them. They're constantly worrying about something they call "Jewish continuity." And you can't say anything critical about Israel in front of them. On the other hand, there's a large group of the non-organized, generally younger people, who perhaps remember something from their childhood—bagels, shabbes candles, a few Yiddish words—but they either live far from the Jewish population centers, or they find nothing amid the existing possibilities that speaks to them.

EJ: You've made secular Yiddish culture both the subject of your studies and your identity. The subject of one's studies is also always to some degree the product of projection ...

MS: First of all, Yiddish culture is only a part of my studies and my identity. The other part is Polish-language Jewish culture. In fact, Polish is more intimately mine than Yiddish. If you add Polish to Yiddish, then yes,

---

16 Agata Kondrat, "Nikt nie mówi dzisiaj w jidysz?," *Cwiszn*, 2010 (1–2), p. 63.

you're right. What do we know today of that world, what can we know? Our knowledge of it will grow, but we'll never be able to experience it from inside. My thesis adviser Rothenberg came from there, he was born and raised there. He knew virtually everything. I know a small fragment of what he knew. Those who come after me will know even less. This world will increasingly recede, the image of this world will be increasingly transformed, and we will transmit some truth and some of our own imagination. So your notion of projection makes some sense. Yet someone still needs this world, someone wants to hear about this culture, someone wants to look at it. In Poland today this is generally truer than elsewhere.

EJ: Your comrades of *No Separate Peace* were part of groups that existed, that fought for real political, economic, and social interests. You, constructing your belongingness, have chosen a group that doesn't exist, doesn't interact with anyone, demands nothing.

MS: That's right! This contradiction is basic. I decided to identify with no longer living Jews and their no longer existing world. I'm not asking anyone to follow me. It's my own choice and my own path. In essence it's a third road beyond Americanization and Israel. The culture of Polish Jews no longer exists. Not because of any fault of its own. Only traces of Polish Jews remain in the place where they lived for centuries. A handful of people remain and what it was possible to transport to America and to Israel. In this I recognized a thing most interesting and valuable. But in the course of time, I see that I'm less and less alone. And it's young people, especially in Poland, that approach these things with great enthusiasm. Who knows what it will bring?

My book *Bondage to the Dead* doesn't much enter into this because it's basically all about Poles. It's a story about servitude, slavery, subservience on the part of Poles, but I don't want my entire life to serve Poles, that is, to be dependent on Poles. At a certain moment I decided to leave this Polish Poland, to no longer dig into this history. Based in my study of Mark Arnshteyn, I returned to prewar Jewish theater—in Yiddish and in Polish. I became theater editor of the *YIVO Encyclopedia of Jewish Life in Eastern Europe.*[17]

---

17 2 vols. (New Haven: Yale University Press, 2008), http://www.yivoencyclopedia.org

The great Yiddish poet Avrom Sutzkever—who began in the same prewar literary group, Yung Vilne, as Shloyme Belis—emphasized the unity and continuity of Jewish culture. He didn't situate his own work in opposition to the works of biblical and rabbinical literature but saw modern secular Jewish literature as only the most recent part of *di goldene keyt*—the golden chain—of Jewish creativity. This was the title of Peretz's play about four generations of a Hasidic family, and it was the title that Sutzkever chose for the literary periodical he launched in Israel after the Holocaust. In some way, through the work I do, I hope to be a tiny part of this whole.

EJ: The idea of parting from Polish Poland seems convincing, but *Bondage to the Dead* doesn't close the matter. Just the opposite. After reading it, there's more and more Polish Poland without end.

Chapter 6

Bondage to the Dead,
First Time Around

Front and back cover: *Bondage to the Dead: Poland and the Memory of the Holocaust*, Syracuse University Press, 1997. Cover art: Susan Erony, *Tower of Babel II*. Phot. Elżbieta Janicka.

EJ: Let's return to the moment when the idea first came to you of writing *Bondage to the Dead*.

MS: In 1983, I looked at Poland from the perspective of an external observer and I saw that people didn't have much of a sense of Polish

Jewish history. Those who wrote about Jewish matters in underground papers searched pretty blindly, found various pieces which they weren't able to put into context. One such piece was 1968 for example. All sorts of things remained unspoken. What was lacking, I felt, was a look at the whole. I've always felt most comfortable thinking synthetically, so I decided to give it a try. At the invitation in the '80s of Charles Rosenzveig, a rabbi in Michigan, I had already published a long article in a volume he edited entitled *The World Reacts to the Holocaust*.[1] Some of its readers suggested that what I had written was already a short book. So at the time I thought it might be good to expand it. When I was still in Poland as a Fulbright Scholar, I was able to send large amounts of material to the States by way of the American Embassy. My good friends Jack LeVert and Cindy Ballenger received many boxes of these materials at their home near Boston. After I returned, Jurek Halbersztadt greatly helped me with clippings from the Polish press. For months I would receive fat envelopes from him filled with articles from Polish newspapers, among which I also found texts on violence against the Roma, which journalists called pogroms. I was up to date. I saw these were the burning issues in Poland.

My personal situation was ideal for doing the work. I had married Meri Adelman, an artist who understood what I was doing and was entirely supportive. Soon our first son Zev was born. I policed his birth and resisted my dybbuk's attempt to sneak into a new home. Zev was an inspiration. I was able to dive into the writing with powerful energy.

EJ: In your book, two currents, two ways of thinking, take center stage—differing from each other, if not conflicting and indeed contradictory, excluding each other. On one hand there's the reconstruction of events—not only accurate but also penetrating to such a degree that it loses nothing of its accuracy in the light of the most recent findings. The original English version of the book appeared in 1997, but if we wanted to update it, Gross's books, the debate about Jedwabne, and current Polish research on the Holocaust could all be put into a footnote.[2] The

---

1   "Poland" in David Wyman, ed. and Charles H. Rosenzveig, project director (Baltimore and London: Johns Hopkins University Press, 1996), pp. 81–155.

2   *Bondage to the Dead* was published in Polish in 2001. Gross's *Neighbors: The Destruction of the Jewish Community in Jedwabne, Poland* was published in Polish in 2000, in English in 2001 (Princeton, N.J.: Princeton University Press). Gross's book, about the murder by

growth of knowledge after 2000 has added additional examples to your observations, but it has in no way affected the basic picture you present. To this, however, you've linked an interpretation that—speaking most cautiously—does not accord with the factual material you present. In our first phone conversation in the spring of this year, you mentioned that from the beginning you had doubts about the notion of the Polish experience of the Holocaust as collective trauma. We promised at that time that we'd discuss this when you came to Warsaw.

MS: I had doubts. I had doubts about Lifton himself, and especially about whether his approach could be applied to the Polish situation.[3] I have to say … that moment, when I began to learn how those who hid Jews were treated after the war … that some of them, even months after the end of the war, did not let these Jews out because they feared for their lives—and for their own lives. There was one person who for nine months did not have the opportunity to safely lead out of his attic … two children. There was a bomb attack on a Jewish orphanage in Rabka. On an orphanage! Michał Borwicz devoted attention to this. A fine scholar. A fine human being. When I was at my aunt and uncle's in Paris, I asked to meet him,

---

Poles of hundreds of Jews in the town of Jedwabne in 1941, seemed to totally transform the discourse about Poles and Jews during World War II, forcing public attention into the so-called dark corners of Polish history, undermining the narrative that Poles have always been only heroes or martyrs. For an introduction to the debate: Antony Polonsky and Joanna Michlic, eds., *The Neighbors Respond: The Controversy Over the Jedwabne Massacre in Poland* (Princeton, N.J.: Princeton University Press, 2004). Subsequent studies of the Polish "dark corners" include two more books by Gross: *Fear: Anti-Semitism in Poland after Auschwitz: An Essay in Historical Interpretation* (New York: Random House, 2006); with Irena Grudzińska-Gross, *Golden Harvest: Events at the Periphery of the Holocaust* (Oxford: Oxford University Press, 2012). See also important studies by Jan Grabowski, *Hunt for the Jews: Betrayal and Murder in German-Occupied Poland* (Bloomington, Ind.: Indiana University Press, 2013) and *Na posterunku: Udział polskiej policji granatowej i kryminalnej w zagładzie Żydów* (Wołowiec: Wydawnictwo Czarne, 2020); and Barbara Engelking, *Such a Beautiful Sunny Day …: Jews Seeking Refuge in the Polish Countryside, 1942–45* (Jerusalem: Yad Vashem, 2016). And see the massive recent study: Barbara Engelking and Jan Grabowski, eds., *Dalej jest noc: Losy Żydów w wybranych powiatach okupowanej Polski* (Warsaw: Stowarzyszenie Centrum Badań nad Zagładą Żydów, 2018), 2 vols.

3   Robert Jay Lifton, *The Broken Connection: On Death and the Continuity of Life* (New York: Basic Books, 1979). Lifton develops the notion of mass trauma induced in witnesses of massive death, such as survivors of the nuclear blast at Hiroshima. The notion of mass trauma is central to the argument in *Bondage to the Dead.*

but we were unable to talk about this. We sat in a café, others at our table too, and drank coffee. Because really, what is there to talk about here? There's nothing to talk about! I couldn't understand and I still can't, how a person, how a human being can do such a thing … It's beyond human comprehension. Just as in the biblical formula "It passeth understanding." I checked, it comes from the New Testament, so it was Christians in fact who thought it up. And there it refers to peace. Not here though. And you know, when I finished writing the piece for Rosenzveig's volume, I sent it to Miłosz.[4] Later we spoke on the phone. And it was the same for Miłosz. He said the text was very good, very clear, but finally he still didn't understand … Of course, I knew what was going on here, but to such an extreme? Because what did I understand from all this? I understood that Poles didn't want to give back Jewish houses, Jewish stuff, so when the Jew returned—a bullet in the head.

EJ: But doesn't it seem to you that you're switching cause and effect? We're murdering the Jew not because we don't want to return his house, but we don't want to return his house because he's a Jew and therefore has no right to live. He doesn't have the right to live in general or—in an immensely merciful Polish version—he doesn't have the right to live *among us*. Except that from the point of view of the murdered, it somehow didn't make a difference and the outcome was always the same. To answer your question: recognizing antisemitism as a cause of these things renders them understandable.

MS: That's a very tough way to see it. I'm not convinced. But I want to say that this we can still somehow comprehend. But that a Pole who hid a Jew had to continue to hide the fact that he hid him? And then the relationship to children for me is …

EJ: And you never heard a response to a question about children? [Long silence.] Your mother also never heard a response to this question?

MS: But don't forget that the first one on that roof still had pity on the children … In any case, I thought to myself that I needed to explain this somehow, make sense of it. I needed to understand it somehow. I knew

---

4   Czesław Miłosz (1911–2004), Nobel Prize winning Polish poet.

about antisemitism before the war and during it. I knew what Karski had written. I read Engel. I read Gutman and Krakowski.[5]

EJ: Engel's disclosure of Karski's memorandum was in 1983. In Poland, it was Gross who published it. Nine years after Engel.[6] But let's say clearly that we're not talking about a document from 1942 known as "Karski's Report," with which Karski had very little or nothing to do. It's a question of Karski's report from December 1939, "The Jewish Issue in Poland under the Occupations," falsified by the author at the request of the Polish government in Angers in the parts concerning the attitudes of Poles to Jews. The following fragments come from the original report: "'The resolution of the Jewish question' by the Germans—I must affirm this with the entire feeling of responsibility for what I am saying—is a serious and quite dangerous instrument in the hands of the Germans for the 'moral pacification' of broad strata of Polish society. [...] The nation detests its deadly foe [i. e. the Germans]—yet this issue ["resolution of the Jewish question"] creates something in the nature of a narrow bridge on which Germans and a large part of Polish society meet in agreement." Karski's falsification did not consist in a simple removal of the parts in question, but their substitution with passages of a precisely opposite meaning, flattering to the majority group. In Poland this material appeared in 1992 in the monthly *Mówią wieki* and passed unnoticed.

MS: I knew about this earlier. I knew what the Polish underground wrote, that there was no more room for Jews and that Poles would not stand with folded arms in the event that some Jews tried to return. I knew

---

5   See David Engel, *In the Shadow of Auschwitz: The Polish Government-in-Exile and the Jews, 1939–1942* (Chapel Hill: University of North Carolina Press, 1987) and *Facing a Holocaust: The Polish Government-in-Exile and the Jews, 1943–1945* (Chapel Hill: University of North Carolina Press, 1993); Israel Gutman and Shmuel Krakowski, *Unequal Victims: Poles and Jews During World War II* (New York: Holocaust Library, 1986).

6   Jan Karski was a courier in the Polish underground who was taken by the Jewish underground to the Warsaw ghetto in 1942, then left for London and Washington where he related what he had seen, though to little effect. The report cited here, however, dates back to December 1939. Jan Gross, "Raport Jana Karskiego o stosunkach polsko-żydowskich w czasie wojny," *Mówią wieki* [Centuries Speak] 4 (202), 1992, p. 2, followed by Karski's "Zagadnienie żydowskie w Polsce pod okupacjami," pp. 3–8.

that people believed in those stories about the Crucifixion, about the *Żydokomuna* [Jew-Commie conspiracy] … But there always remained something that didn't fit into my head. All the time I thought, felt, was convinced, that I was missing something, that there had to be something more, an additional reason, which would allow me to understand how what happened after the war was possible.

EJ: If there existed a contest for the saddest letter, your letters to me would compete with one another for first prize. Listen: "I stood before a historical situation that I believed to be unacceptable. Namely, the attitude to Jews on the part of those closest to them, who saw everything the Germans did to them up close, did not change after the war. In fact, it got worse. In order to understand this, in order to save some notion of humanity, of humankind, in order to contest the views with which I was raised, that Poles were worse than the Germans, for a long time I looked for some way out, some new, unknown perspective, and that's how I reached Lifton. And then it felt as though I'd lifted a weight from my soul."[7]

MS: Yes. I was able to deal with it then.

EJ: You lifted a weight from your soul. Except that you can lift it, but you can't heave it away. You look at the Holocaust through the eyes of a person for whom the Holocaust is a tragedy. And you don't want to see or know that there could exist people—even entire societies and cultures—for whom the Holocaust was not a tragedy, to say the least. In order to continue not seeing and knowing what you see and know so well, you dole out your own trauma to everyone. You provide them with your own wound, regardless of their attitude or behavior. In other words, regardless of the place they occupied in the structure of the crime. You ignore their perspective. It looks as though you're colonizing the subject of your study. But a graduate of Columbia doesn't colonize the subject of his study because that's what a Columbia education should have taught him to avoid. So *de facto*, it's not colonization of the subject of study but flight from the subject of study. Because of the lack of physical and psychic possibilities to endure it. I'm speaking descriptively and not making a value judgment.

---

7   Letter to Elżbieta Janicka, June 19, 2014.

MS: I have to admit that in the light of the most recent studies of your historians, things have started to look different. What's changed, and perhaps even, as you write, what's become outdated, is the notion of the Polish witness and Polish witnessing of the Holocaust. For a new edition of the book, this is something I'd certainly consider. But you also must understand that I wrote the book for Americans and American Jews as well as for Poles. The American opinion of Poles is not good. Poles are considered antisemites. I fight against this.

EJ: But you're not a lobbyist, you're an intellectual. And really, recent research hasn't introduced any qualitative changes in your representation of the Holocaust in *Bondage*.

MS: I was also concerned not to write only about the war, to recall the whole history of Jews in Poland. Because it wasn't as if Jews sat here on their valises for centuries. Look at those giant synagogues, first wooden, then masonry—those weren't temporary installations, they were built over generations. There was time for this, there was money. Such structures were not raised by some persecuted group of people hovering on the edge of survival. Certainly, the peasant constantly heard in church that the Jews killed God and so on, but day to day this hardly got in the way.

EJ: It didn't get in the way of Christians?

MS: It didn't get in the way of Jews!

EJ: Well, sure. Here a little pogrom, there a little trial, elsewhere a little stake. Ransoms as an everyday thing. *De non tolerandis Judaeis.* In the larger cities forced relocations. In Warsaw, still in the nineteenth century, you bet! In the medieval university city of Kraków, daily violence committed against the Jews by students. A detail. Let's agree that in the Commonwealth, conditions for Jews were better than elsewhere, but still let's not say that all this didn't get in the way for Jews. And let's not call this *Paradisus Judaeorum*,[8] because the term comes from an antisemitic pamphlet. Today's version of the term is *Judaeopolonia.*

---

8   Jewish Paradise, term used for centuries by antisemites to describe the alleged Jewish domination of Poland.

MS: Your words are dark, cold and hard. Of course, not only yours. I've encountered similar takes—entirely new for me—among some younger scholars of our matters. I've been thinking about it. There's something to it. But to a certain degree, I also consider it an exaggeration. Look, in the Commonwealth, Jews had far-ranging autonomy, various forms of self-government. The Council of the Four Lands was active.[9]

EJ: Am I saying that they didn't have far-ranging autonomy, self-government, the Council of the Four Lands? The king allowed this in order to assure his enterprise, which was the state, more efficient tax collection. And to the extent that he could, he shielded the Jews from the Church, defending the interests of the state, because it was Jews who built that state. He could count on their loyalty, competence, and money, in a situation in which, except for them, there were few he could rely on. It wasn't Christian compassion or Old Polish hospitality that motivated him, but rational calculation. And it wasn't because of Polish patriotism that Dov Ber Meisels exhorted prayers for Polish success in the battles against Russia, and later supported the Spring of Nations.[10] What I argue for is the rational use of language, the discarding of mystified categories of description.

MS: I agree. It wasn't a question here of philosemitism or philopolonism. But let's also remember that besides the kings, there were magnate-owned tracts [*jurydyki*] where Jews were allowed to settle and could feel relatively safe.

EJ: "Philosemitism—philopolonism." Help! A mystified pair of mystified terms. Symmetrical construction suggesting the equal status of the dominant and the subordinate group. The mirror image of the pair: "antisemitism—antipolonism." And everything generated by the refusal to confront antisemitism. It goes like this: we've got antisemitism, so we make up something called antipolonism. In other words, to the actual phenomenon we tag on "for balance" an imaginary phenomenon. Thanks to this, racist,

---

9   Supreme governing body of the Polish Jewish community, 1580–1764.
10 Dov Ber Meisels (1798–1870), influential rabbi of the Jewish communities of Kraków and Warsaw, he supported the Polish uprisings and was considered a Polish patriot by Poles.

religiously sanctioned, and morally rationalized hatred of the minority by the majority can be described using the terms of intergroup conflict, and antisemitism is rationalized. Such a tactic of opposition to knowledge and self-knowledge can be understood on the part of the culture that practices violence, but on the part of the culture that is subject to violence? Not mentioning that the opposite of antisemitism isn't philosemitism. Sandauer, for example, in the text you value, showed their common allosemitic origin. You know all this. Why then do you say such things?

MS: What? That I put philosemitism and philopolonism on the same level and what's worse, antisemitism and antipolonism? Where do I suggest such an equivalence? Not in the least. But here's a question. Why, when a young Pole travels outside of Poland and says he's a Pole, why does he often hear the response: "So you're an antisemite?"

EJ: A complete puzzle. If you look at Polish opinion polls and the walls of Polish cities, you really don't know what it's about. We must defend our Pole, pre-emptively is best, even before he's addressed with the question, which moreover he's generally rarely asked. By himself, the poor thing won't know what to answer. He'll certainly be freed from his oppression by the legend of King Casimir the Great.[11] And it won't hurt to add Count Potocki.[12] But let's return to the magnate-owned lands. Yes, as you say, there were magnate-owned tracts where Jews were allowed to settle and could feel relatively safe. But now look at the intellectual construction we've gotten to as a result. The question concerned the reputation of Poles in the United States, but the answer deals with the Council of the Four Lands and magnate-owned tracts. What does this have to do with the reputation of Poles? What does this have to do with Poles at all?

MS: Agreed. We're speaking of royal and magnate authorities, later also local nobility, that is, the landowners who well understood their interests. There was no Polish nation then, this was the pre-national era. When national ideas developed, things looked less good for Jews, even those

---

11 King Casimir the Great (1310–70) is believed to have "invited" Jews to settle in Poland.

12 Count Walentyn Potocki, fictional eighteenth-century Polish nobleman who is said to have converted to Judaism and therefore been burnt at the stake.

who wanted to stop being Jews because they believed there was something wrong with it. All true. It was an unequal exchange of services, not a matter of Polish merits. And there was no question here of anyone wanting to be nice to the Jews. But this was all in the Commonwealth…[13]

EJ: Where the victims of the system were the peasants, whose descendants consider themselves today—as nearly everyone here—as the inheritors of that state and as benefactors of the Jews. It's all based on a culture in which tolerating Jews in a subordinate position and for one's own interests is understood as beneficence. And you owe gratitude to your benefactor, without looking into the actual state of affairs: the historical relation of the majority culture to Jews and the relation of the majority of Polish society to Jews before, during and after the war. This makes sense psychologically, but it's entirely false epistemologically. But we've unnecessarily taken a detour.

Regardless of the false logic of this discourse, a characteristic pattern is embedded in it. That is: the better the situation of Jews, the more their situation depends on Polish behavior; the worse the situation of Jews, the weaker the link to the Polish environment—until that connection is totally severed during the Holocaust. In that way, for Poles, the Holocaust becomes extraterritorial—an event played out between Jews and Germans in a social void.

MS: Agreed. That's what I write.

EJ: I would say it appears for you rather in the interpretive sphere. Moreover, Christianity and the Church are lacking in your book, except perhaps in a scattered subliminal way.

MS: The king, the magnates, and the nobility needed the Jews. The peasants were incapacitated by the system, which secured the interests of king, magnates, and nobles. The only actually dangerous enemy in this situation was the Church. In the eighteenth century, this was no longer a joke.

EJ: But you don't write about this in the book.

---

13 1569–1795; also known as the Commonwealth of Poland and Lithuania.

MS: There's a lot I don't write about. The history of Polish-Jewish relations until the interwar period is contained in one short chapter. And certainly, with such an approach, the question of the formation of majority identity in opposition to the Jews—both in the pre-national period as in the national—gets lost.

EJ: Later on, you also don't write about the Church, except for little touches here and there.

MS: I mention it for example in relation to the Kielce pogrom.[14]

EJ: That's exactly what I mean by little touches. In Polish public and academic discourse, there's a ritual which consists of keeping the investigator from conclusions of a more general nature. This type of conclusion is discredited as a "rash generalization." This is one of the techniques for blocking debate, because without "rash generalizations" we never get beyond the limits of fragmentary evidence, and the problem is gone. With you those "rash generalizations" are there, but never in relation to the doctrine or the institution of the Catholic Church. The result is that we get an image that even in part doesn't reflect the power—and this not only material, however material too, but above all mental and emotional—of the Church. One can completely forget that things are happening in a country dominated by Christian culture, not to mention that we never learn what Christianity meant for the Jews. The way you tell it, antisemitism is never problematized. Yet you're a specialist in that field. Was this in fact some sort of self-censorship on your part?

MS: I don't know. In a new edition, I'd add some sentences in the first chapter.

EJ: And in each succeeding one?

---

14 The notorious murder of more than forty Holocaust survivors and the wounding of over forty more in Kielce on July 4, 1946, caused most Jews to decide that there was no future for them in Poland. See Joanna Tokarska-Bakir, *Pod klątwą. Społeczny portret pogromu kieleckiego*, 2 vols. (Warsaw: Czarna Owca, 2018).

MS: But I do write about the relation of the Church to Jews in the inter-war period.

EJ: You do on the basis of suggesting Jewish responsibility for the attitude and behavior of the Church. Perhaps I exaggerate, but the responsibility of the Church here vanishes. In the body of the text, you write that the Church condemned hatred and violence against Jews. But in the foot-note—at the end of the chapter in the Polish version and in the English one at very end of the book—you cite Modras' study arguing that the Polish Church's strongly antisemitic teachings during this period were not exceptional, "but were entirely in line with those of the Church else-where in Europe and with the rhetoric of the Vatican." And you add, "But nowhere else in Europe did the Church confront 3.5 million Jews."[15]

MS: In the main text, I write that the Church condemned hatred, but in the next sentence I add, ironically, that this did not prevent the Church from conducting a "'moral' struggle against [...] Jewish atheism, Bolshevism, pornography, and fraud"[16] as well as encouraging boycotts of Jewish businesses.

EJ: Your book is entirely lacking in irony which is why it's impossible to realize that this one sentence is ironic.

MS: There are other ironies in the book. Moreover, you're focusing an inquisition on the interwar period, a section that totals eight pages.

EJ: Was there something that kept you from speaking straightforwardly?

MS: Perhaps the powerful example of John Paul. Remember when this was written: in the early years of the '90s. Agreed, that what he said about Jews was not entirely decent. There was still Catholic or Christian tri-umphalism in his thinking, but I was impressed by how he conquered the Communists with their own weapon. We've spoken of this already. Dignity of labor, humanity, universal values …

---

15 *Bondage to the Dead*, pp. 21, 151; Ronald Modras, *The Catholic Church and Antisemitism: Poland, 1933–1939* (Amsterdam: Harwood, 1994).
16 *Bondage*, p. 21.

EJ: Under the cross.

MS: My Polish Jewish comrades didn't believe in the cross, yet they stood under it. They stood with John Paul.

EJ: Who defined the Polish nation …

MS: As a Christian nation. He would also talk about the soil. That the Polish soil was this or that. He didn't understand how dangerous this was. But there was no enmity there. Towards anyone.

EJ: And so accordingly, in 1979 the "Polish Pope" celebrated a holy Catholic mass under a cross placed next to a white and red flag at the ramp at Birkenau. And as to how to define the nation, once set in motion, John Paul's definition produces violence and exclusion. Such are its underlying assumptions.

MS: What we need of course is an integrated history. Here I agree with you entirely, because as you've written, until now, instead of a history of Poland we have the history of Poles.[17]

EJ: The first to say this in Poland was Feliks Tych. It was he who appealed at the end of the '90s for an "integrated, complete history of the multinational society part of which constituted Jews. But as far as Polish historiography goes, the specific problem is that it presented until recently (and to a large extent still does) a history of Poland nearly entirely from the point of view of the ruling nation, even though Poland was always, until 1939, a multinational state."[18] I know that on a microscale, this is what Mark Mazower did for Salonika.[19]

---

17 Elżbieta Janicka, "Pamięć przyswojona. Koncepcja polskiego doświadczenia zagłady Żydów jako traumy zbiorowej w świetle rewizji kategorii świadka," *Studia Litteraria et Historica*, 2014-15 (3-4), pp. 148–226, https://ispan.waw.pl/journals/index.php/slh/article/view/slh.2015.009/1628; "O nowe kategorie opisu. W odpowiedzi Janowi Grabowskiemu," *Zagłada Żydów*, 2012 (8), pp. 468–474.

18 Feliks Tych, *Długi cień Zagłady. Szkice historyczne* (Warsaw: Żydowski Instytut Historyczny, 1999), p. 144. Tych (1929–2015) was the director of the Jewish Historical Institute, 1995–2006.

19 *Salonica, City of Ghosts: Christians, Muslims and Jews 1430-1950* (New York: HarperCollins, 2004).

MS: Nor is this impossible on a macroscale. There's an integrated history of Ukraine that's been published in English where the history of the Jews might have been better written, but it's there.[20]

EJ: I don't know this book. But an integrated history is not a history of the majority with "minority corners" graciously added, as they do in Polish museums and schools. It's a history, certainly, of various groups, but also of their intersecting situations and relations—not necessarily mutual, since sometimes the disproportion between the dominating and the dominated is so great that to speak of any sort of mutuality would falsify reality. Małgorzata Melchior has noticed this, questioning the validity of the category "Polish-Jewish relations" in reference to what happened between Poles and Jews in occupied Poland.[21] An integrated history is to a large extent a history of violence and exclusion. And to approach it, we first have to integrate the history of the majority, that is, supplement it with what today isn't in it: what the majority of this majority can't wrap its mind around.

MS: This will be the next achievement.

EJ: In Poland, we are systematically retreating from this moment because of an exclusionary and violent identity and historical politics.

MS: Yet isn't it the case that today Poles are capable of taking in more than they were able to take in fifteen years ago?

EJ: Agreed, as far as that goes. But the question is whether this disturbs the prevailing organization of knowledge or whether it only strengthens it. What narrative does it inscribe itself into? One leading to a revision of notions, attachments, and loyalties, directly leading to the conclusion that we have to reimagine ourselves as a community that is finally political and—horrors!—based in citizenship.

---

20 Paul Robert Magocsi, *A History of Ukraine* (Seattle: University of Washington, 1996).

21 Małgorzata Melchior, "Socjologiczne pojęcia i kategorie do opisu stosunków polsko-żydowskich w czasie okupacji," in Katedra Socjologii i Antropologii Obyczajów i Prawa ISNS UW, ed., *O społeczeństwie, prawie i obyczajach. Księga pamiątkowa ofiarowana profesorowi Jackowi Kurczewskiemu* (Gdańsk: słowo/obraz terytoria, 2013), pp. 386–96.

MS: In your opinion, do the ravages of the Holocaust extend that far? [Silence.] The most recent historical findings indeed look like the nail in the coffin, as far as that goes.

EJ: As though there was not enough before. Since based on the historiography of the Holocaust in occupied Poland—produced for years beyond Polish borders—is this actually a Copernican revolution? Is this a revolution of any kind? Studies in Poland have only begun. The growth of factual knowledge is so rapid that it's impossible to completely assess its meaning for our understanding of what happened. But when I read various old works by Borwicz, Datner, Gutman, Krakowski or Engel, it's hard for me to think of today's work as pioneering.

MS: Listen, I'm an American Polish Jew, of which the most important part is nevertheless the American. I'm an American. And as an American I don't believe and I won't believe, I can't believe, I don't want to believe what Karski wrote about the narrow bridge on which Poles and Germans met about the Jews.

EJ: Because it signifies breaking the human spine.

MS: Precisely! As an American I have this belief in humanity—in the humanity of the human, in humanness—which not only excludes such a thing but excludes the very possibility of thinking it.

EJ: I understand that what spoke out of you was not paternalism and hidden contempt. That the notion of the Polish experience of the Holocaust as trauma was not a handout for Poles, but an attempt to save your own belief in the most basic of basics, right?

MS: A bit of diplomacy may have been there, but essentially it wasn't about diplomacy. It was about saving the minimum, salvaging a space in which we can still be human.

EJ: Because that maneuver with trauma could have been received—as I received it—as setting things up in such a way that Poles had to be treated as Poles. Everyone sees what the Pole is like. Poles are Poles and can't do more than they can. They can't and they won't be able to. A conversation of equals with them will never be possible, so instead of treating them like everyone else, we should be pleased that—and here the ritual formula which makes me break out in hives: "For Poland, it's not bad [Jak na Polskę, to nieźle]."

MS: No, above all I wanted to save a belief in meaning … the possibility of belief in the possibility of meaning.

EJ: But maybe we don't have to give up on it? Maybe just orient it forward and not project it back. What happened can't be reversed. We have no influence over it. We can only influence what we do with it now. With it and because of it. That actually depends on us. The possibility I'm speaking of isn't pessimistic. It's based on taking responsibility and recovering what's called *agency*, that is, turning oneself from object into active human subject. Without it there can be no mutual subjectivation. Because you can't treat another as subject without treating yourself as one.

MS: How can I believe that people on a bus or trolley or train are able to say, well, Hitler, whatever, but he did one good thing, and that was cleaning up the Jews?

EJ: They know they won't be stigmatized. And those who it wounds know they can't say anything. So it's about social and cultural legitimacy and the lack of such legitimacy.

MS: And that is the question!

EJ: Is it a question or is it an answer?

MS: Still a question, I'd say. Really, reading you and other young Polish historians, I'm starting to have doubts about some of my assumptions. Tomek Pietrasiewicz, the founder of Grodzka Gate in Lublin, is trying to convince me to come out with a new edition of the book. For that matter, not only he.[22] After years, certainly, the book needs updating.

---

22 Tomasz Pietrasiewicz is the founder and director of Brama Grodzka [Grodzka Gate], an institution dedicated to constructing the memory of the Jews of Lublin.

Bondage to the Dead ends after all on the fiftieth anniversary of the liberation of Oświęcim—or as we say now, Auschwitz-Birkenau. So, first of all, I'd have to add a final chapter devoted to Gross's book and the reactions that it provoked. The publication of *Neighbors* and the Jedwabne debate, it seems to me, were the Polish equivalent of the Dreyfus Affair. Next—and this will be harder—I'd need to revise the underlying assumptions, the conceptual framework of the book. I'd have to return to the third chapter and address the theory of trauma and the category of witness. This requires some more thought, but I'm inclined to agree with you about eliminating the traumatic interpretation which doesn't work here in its present form. And that word witness at least needs to have quotation marks around it. Most important at this moment is to try to answer the question of what the newest Polish research means for our understanding of the subject. I'm just afraid of the reaction of the American reader who will say "Well, yes, we know all this, we've known it all along."

EJ: "'How horrible!' cried Lara, for she is not without a heart."[23] This is Lara Croft, of course.

MS: I must commend you on starting to turn to popular culture. You will admit it's pretty useful.

EJ: Does that "American reader" you talk about have something in common with the phantasmatic "New York Jews"? Because Adam Michnik likes to use them as bogeymen when he runs out of arguments. Sometimes he can even call you to talk and then announce: "You don't know what you're saying, writing, and playing with. You don't know New York Jews!" This is Adam Michnik who at every opportunity announces: "The Pole of Jewish descent—such as I—carries an additional responsibility of fighting the stereotype of the Pole as a 'genetic antisemite.' [...] It's the reason for my really very firm polemics with the Jewish community in America and Europe, where this stereotype is powerfully rooted."[24] This genetic antisemitism business is intellectually dishonest because none of the participants in the debate—with Yitzkhak Shamir

---

23 "Lara Croft" in Bożena Keff, *On Mother and Fatherland*, trans. from the Polish by Benjamin Paloff and Alissa Valles (Asheville, N.C.: MadHat Press, 2017), p. 12.
24 Marek Beylin, "Tak mówią dysydenci," *Gazeta Wyborcza*, June 21–22, 2014, p. 25.

at the head[25]—have claimed, nor do they claim, anything comparable. It's not about genetic coding. It's about cultural coding. About socialization. Curious that from the point of view of the wounded and the maddened, it's the damage to Polish reputation that's so painful. At the same time, it escapes their notice that Polish neighbors robbed and murdered Shamir's family. Shamir dug his father's headless corpse out of the family garden. But there's somehow no room for this in the story of this archetypical hater of Poles.

MS: I admit that I didn't know about Shamir's family. I understand better now where his comment came from. Still, I have to return to that young Polish traveler who doesn't understand why he—and not a German for instance—is considered a born antisemite.

EJ: That happens because the planet has been overcome by an anti-Polish conspiracy. Simple. But seriously? You yourself explain in *Bondage to the Dead* the principle of the polonocentric perspective in which the Holocaust was "transformed affectively into a German-Jewish plot against Poles. [...] The meaning of the Holocaust had become Polish victimization *by* the Holocaust."[26] I agree with you completely as far as that goes. That's exactly the world I was born into and in which I grew up.

MS: In the book, my comment applied to the craziness of government propaganda in 1968. I guess I didn't realize how deeply it reflected popular consciousness after all, and how long it lasted—down to the present, as we're starting to see.

---

25 In 1989 Shamir became notorious in Poland for having said that Poles suck in antisemitism with their mother's milk.
26 *Bondage to the Dead*, pp. 85–86.

Chapter 7

Bondage to the Dead,
Second Time Around

Front and back cover: *Pamięć nieprzyswojona. Polska pamięć Zagłady* [Unmastered Memory: Polish Memory of the Holocaust], translated into Polish by Agata Tomaszewska and Agata Patalas (Warsaw: Wydawnictwo Cyklady, 2001). Cover photograph: Monika Krajewska. Phot. Elżbieta Janicka.

The image is a graphically altered portion of a photograph of the Jewish cemetery in Karczew taken by Monika Krajewska; it originally appeared in her album *Czas kamieni* [Time of Stones] (Warsaw: Interpress, 1982), p. 59, which in the 1980s gained a cult following.

MS: It was surprising for me, and still is, that none of my friends, those who were working to renew Jewish life in the '80s, expressed any interest in the book. They were my guides. I learned what Poland is from them. I'll admit that I was impatient to see what they would say. These are all people who write and publish. Meanwhile not one of them responded. There was no discussion. The book appeared and then disappeared. Did they feel it wasn't worth their commentary? But I had written about our common matters. Until today I don't understand this.

EJ: I've been thinking about this too.

MS: It's a bigger issue. It's not about a single person, but about a group. I'd say that—besides Jurek Halbersztadt—those who were important in my writing included Paweł Śpiewak, Staszek Krajewski and Kostek Gebert. Kostek offered me material from his vast collection of underground publications. This was the basis on which I later wrote about Solidarity's relations with Jews. I talked for many hours, if not days, with them, about all these things. Then I present my work and nothing, silence. Silence after the English edition appeared, silence after the Polish one.

EJ: The Polish edition overlapped with the publication of Gross's *Neighbors* which was also ignored for some time by the leading intellectual centers including, programmatically, by *Gazeta Wyborcza*. It was some local press and not so well-known journalistic voices that wouldn't let go and stuck with the subject. Later, the debate about *Neighbors* eclipsed everything else.

MS: But the English edition of my book came out in 1997, and these were all people who knew English perfectly. A year later *Gazeta Wyborcza* published the chapter on the postwar period in their own translation.[1] Zero reaction.

---

1 "Rany pamięci [Memory's wounds] 1944–1948," trans. by Michał Lipszyc, *Gazeta Wyborcza*, July 4–5, 1998, pp. 22–25. In boldface below the headline: "Poles were only witnesses to the Holocaust, yet nevertheless this induced feelings of guilt toward the Jews. This was so strongly repressed and displaced that it had to manifest itself in a particular, destructive form – writes Michael C. Steinlauf."

EJ: Maybe your book expressed what at that time was self-evident, and in this sense unproblematic? Maybe after reading it, one could feel comfortable and safe? Because the subject isn't safe and isn't comfortable, but here suddenly the reader sees everything rounded out, rationalized, inscribed into a pendulum-like movement under the signs of "yes but" and "nevertheless however." Though I have to admit that I still dream certain things at night, as when you write that the Polish underground state was the first fulfillment in history of the ideal of Poland for Poles. How could something like that be ignored? But perhaps it was deemed that, since in America there was quiet after the publication, in Poland one could also sleep peacefully. Because here what functions is the provincial complex and intellectual sovereignty is rare. This is not about everyone, I stress, but in public debate the argument "What will they say about us abroad?" functions quite seriously. So then if the mythical "abroad" lets the thing go, there's no cause for concern. Generally, though, your book seems to me to function in a self-anaesthetizing way. On the one hand, in many places it transgresses the limits of permissible Polish thinking at the time the book appeared, that is, of the "truth-threshold,"—a term first coined by Feliks Tych.[2] But on the other hand, it neutralizes inconvenient facts with the help of a narrative widely known and liked in Poland.

MS: I was afraid that no one had read my book, but when someone finally read it—you, I mean—I don't know if I'm so pleased either.

EJ: But what did you think, when from Dariusz Stola's review you learned that you gracefully maneuver in the minefield of Polish-Jewish history, thanks to which everyone can stick to their own positions? This was supposed to be a compliment. Though at the same time you were rebuked for insufficiently blaming the Communists—whose victim was also, after all, the Polish nation—for the fate of the Jews after 1945. Stola concluded that—despite your efforts, which he recognized and praised—with you the truth does not lie, as it should, sufficiently in the middle.[3]

---

2   *Długi cień Zagłady*, p. 160.
3   Dariusz Stola, *Holocaust and Genocide Studies*, 1997, 11 (3), pp. 426–431. Stola was the director of the Museum of the History of Polish Jews from 2014–19. He was removed from this position by the right-wing minister of culture. In Poland there

MS: When I hear this now a red light goes on. But back then I worried about readers being able to stand it, finding some way of reading it and then going on to think about the whole.

EJ: Except I'm not sure that from your book it follows that the whole requires further thought. Zofia Wóycicka, who reviewed the Polish version, sees this in fact as the fault of your argument: "The thesis that the source of the rather widespread hatred of Jews in postwar Poland was trauma provoked by witnessing the Holocaust and the resulting feeling of guilt somehow frees Poles of responsibility. [...] In the course of further studies it may well turn out that Steinlauf's image of the Polish attitude to Jews during the war is too positive. [...] When I read the last chapter of Steinlauf's book, another sad reflection occurs to me, that the author also perhaps assessed the future development of the situation in Poland too optimistically."[4]

MS: My intention was to reach Poles as well as Jews.

EJ: And in this way you reached neither Jews nor Poles.

MS: I disagree. And you think that Gross's aggressive approach reached them? We're not talking about Gross now, just about his reception.

EJ: We can agree, then, that aggression in this case is in the eye of the beholder.

MS: Gross says that the process that led to the crime and the crime itself had no justification. Whereas Poles, in their opinion, have a host of motives and complicated circumstances to justify themselves. In this sense, Gross entirely doesn't take into account the attitudes or beliefs of Poles.

---

was also a purely descriptive review of the English edition; see Małgorzata Melchior, "Michael C. Steinlauf, *Bondage to the Dead: Poland and the Memory of the Holocaust*," *Przegląd Socjologiczny* 49 (2000), nr. 2, pp. 232–35.

4 Zofia Wóycicka, "Polacy na kozetce [Poles on the couch], czyli rozważania nad książką Michaela C. Steinlaufa *Pamięć nieprzyswojona*," *Kultura i Społeczeństwo* 3 (2002), pp. 178-79.

EJ: Most Poles. Not all. Gross refuses to recognize rationalization as an explanation, rationalization as a reason.

MS: This is going on the warpath.

EJ: I agree. Talking to Poles like people is a *casus belli*. This is one of the unquestioned accomplishments of Polish dominant culture. Gross rejects discussion on conditions dictated by the Polish majority, though even with him you can find elements of pro-Polish or pro-Christian wishful thinking.[5] But essentially, he thinks and speaks as if he weren't subjected to the symbolic violence of the majority culture. The key example here is a text he published in the celebrated issue of *Aneks* from 1986: "He is from my fatherland … but I don't like him."[6] Scrupulously ignored at the time. The hero of the issue was recognized then to be Aleksander Smolar with his essay "Taboo and Innocence" confirming the dominant majority in its beliefs.[7]

MS: Many Polish—and not only Polish—historians accuse Gross of ignoring context.

EJ: It seems to me he's mainly interested precisely in context—though more social than cultural. But the cultural is there too. Generally, though, after Gross the critique of culture is still to be done—extending what's already been done (for example, by Maria Janion[8]) and what's in progress (the work of Joanna Tokarska-Bakir, for instance[9]). Gross rejects accepting as context what antisemitic narrative presents as context: so-called economic conflict, the so-called Żydokomuna, so-called

---

5   See Elżbieta Janicka, "Mord rytualny z aryjskiego paragrafu. O książce Jana Tomasza Grossa *Strach. Antysemityzm w Polsce tuż po wojnie. Historia moralnej zapaści*," *Kultura i Społeczeństwo* 2 (2008), pp. 229–252.
6   See Jan Gross, "Ten jest z ojczyzny mojej …, ale go nie lubię [He is from my fatherland …, but I don't like him]," *Aneks* 41–42 (1986), pp. 13–36. The title plays on a line of Adam Mickiewicz that most Poles know by heart as well the title of a well-known book by Władysław Bartoszewski and Zofia Lewin about Poles who helped Jews.
7   pp. 89–133.
8   See Maria Janion, *Hero, Conspiracy, and Death: The Jewish Lectures* (Frankfurt am Main: PL Academic Research/Peter Lang, 2014).
9   See Joanna Tokarska-Bakir, *Legendy o krwi. Antropologia przesądu* (Warsaw: W.A.B., 2008).

over-representation. This at least concerns the charges of lack of context that are thrown at Gross in Poland. Majority sensitivities are also outraged whenever the unequal status of majority and minority, that is, the asymmetrical situations of the two groups, is exposed.

MS: Gross's critics also claim that his work lacks nuance.

EJ: It seems to me that here what's applied is the disqualifying mechanism known as "rash generalizations." But we'd have to discuss this with texts in hand. In any case, it seems to me that there is nuance in Gross. On the other hand, as I learned based on my own research, the more nuance, the worse the whole looks.

MS: I guess I wanted to avoid the kind of accusations directed at Gross. Because what's the sense of it? Where does it lead? In such an atmosphere any sort of discussion becomes impossible.

EJ: And that's the essence of the thing! That's precisely what we should be talking about! Patiently identify, show, analyze why and as a result of what mechanisms discussion isn't possible, and what there is, is no discussion. And that this can continue only if the point of view of one side is accepted by both sides as self-evident, transparent, indisputable. The violence must be exposed. If not, we'll never get out of it.

MS: This is a job for you and those like you.

EJ: Maybe I even agree with you, exceptionally. Only that then you and those like you agree about Polin as *Paradisus Judaeorum*. Sorry, you don't deserve that caricature, but "my ending is despair," as Mickey Mouse would say.[10]

MS: Let me tell you something that may make you feel better. Jewish immigrants from Eastern Europe couldn't stand the Jews they found in America. Do you know what they called them? *Allrightniks*. Because when you asked one of them how they're doing, they replied

---

10 Actually, Prospero in Shakespeare's *Tempest*.

"all right." And that's what you're talking about here, right? And now listen. In this whole business, we're touching on one question: continuity or discontinuity? Was the Holocaust a rupture with all prior culture or was it its extension? If the latter, then how to approach those who live in the extension of this extension? And who is anyone to take such a step? You must accept something as valid currency, don't you?

EJ: Valid currency, valid coin, gold coin. Jewish gold. The little Jew with a gold coin! The little Jew with a gold coin who you can buy everywhere in Poland, and who today's Poles—the vast majority—place in their homes in honest belief, of course, for good fortune.

MS: You see yourself. For you the continuity is almost palpable. You even speak of the logical and moral legitimization of the Holocaust in the categories of the dominant culture then and now.

EJ: And I believe there's a way out of this. We are not condemned to this vicious circle. Certainly, I somehow imagine what those of the second generation feel who don't see this or refuse to see it. You belong to the latter, yes? But I'm asking about the consequences of such a position. I'm asking about the consequences, but at the same time I believe that one should always remember and try to talk about the feeling that accompanies this refusal.

MS: For me, it's not a refusal but a recognition of the Holocaust as something unimaginable, as a rupture in history, not only in Polish-Jewish history but in human history as a whole.

EJ: At the same time at Gratz College, you direct a program called Holocaust and Genocide Studies which is necessarily comparative since the discipline of Holocaust and Genocide Studies arose out of reflections on the Holocaust.

MS: Yes, because on the other hand, I insist that the Holocaust happened in history. To understand the Holocaust, you have to study history. Yes. But nevertheless, in these studies you reach a point at which you stop understanding. That's also what Friedländer says over and over in his key work.[11] You approach it, and you reach a point at which you can't find words, any words. I feel that the Holocaust constitutes a fundamental rupture in all of human history.

EJ: People did this.

MS: That's precisely what I can't understand, that—as your writer Zofia Nałkowska puts it—people did this to people.[12]

EJ: But maybe people really wouldn't have done this to people. Henryk Grynberg and Marek Zaleski argued about whether people did this to people or people did it to Jews.[13] Whereas Kinga Dunin wants something more, something that could shock Poles and change attitudes. The word "Jew"– as it's understood in Polish culture – contains an invitation to violence and justification for that violence. For the contents of this word are the antisemitic fantasies embedded in Polish collective thinking. From this perspective the persecution and murder of Jews is part of the natural order of things, in contrast to the persecution and murder of *people*, which is seen as a fundamental violation of that order. That's why, according to Dunin, in Poland we have to repeat that in persecuting and murdering Jews, Poles persecuted and murdered people. In other words, Poles did it to people.[14]

MS: But it was not inevitable.

---

11 See Saul Friedländer, *Nazi Germany and the Jews: The Years of Persecution, 1933–1939* (New York: HarperCollins, 1997) and *Nazi Germany and the Jews: The Years of Extermination* (New York: HarperCollins, 2007).

12 See Zofia Nałkowska, *Medaliony* (Warsaw: Czytelnik, 1946).

13 Henryk Grynberg, "Ludzie Żydom zgotowali ten los," in *Prawda nieartystyczna* (West Berlin: Archipelag, 1984), pp. 65–88; Marek Zaleski, "'Ludzie ludziom' …? 'Ludzie Żydom' …? Świadectwo literatury?" in Alina Brodzka-Wald, Dorota Krawczyńska, and Jacek Leociak, eds., *Literatura polska wobec Zagłady* (Warsaw: ŻIH, 2000), pp. 89–103.

14 See Kinga Dunin, *Czytając Polskę. Literatura polska po roku 1989 wobec dylematów nowoczesności* (Warsaw: W.A.B., 2004), pp. 72–78.

EJ: It was not inevitable. But it was not accidental either. It played out within a specific social fabric, and what was done was done by people who didn't come from Mars but from a specific culture. Putting it that way allows us to inspect that culture and to critique it. Above all it requires that we not reproduce the antisemitic gestures with criminal potential—the jokes, the superstitions, the graffiti. But in Poland, in the realms of identity politics, historical politics, public discourse and education, we still haven't dealt with this, and we've recently regressed in this respect. Scrutiny of the culture has begun, but until now it has had no influence on mainstream thinking.

MS: Poland has changed enormously over the last thirty years. For the better. That's the way it looks in the eyes of an American Jew who loves Warsaw. Fascination with Jewish culture is everywhere and visible to the naked eye.

EJ: Jewish culture or what the majority group imagines is Jewish culture?

MS: The fascination itself is important. You just have to steer it skillfully. Whatever the case, the change is huge in comparison to the situation which I remember from the '80s when there was nothing. But it's far more than that. It's not even a matter of "For Poland it's not bad." The amount of Polish scholarship on Yiddish culture is extraordinary.

EJ: And its quality in terms of critical thinking?

MS: The level of the Kraków festival is actually very high. The musical tastes and cultural competence of Janusz Makuch and his team are impeccable.

EJ: I don't mean the number and quality of the performers, the number of tickets sold or the number of meters of cable needed for the sound system.

MS: I don't know. And I don't know how to measure it. The effect of these performances on the Polish audience is probably not very deep, but the energy they evoke is unambiguously positive. I'm impressed by the very existence of so many Jewish culture festivals in Poland and the fact that they are so enthusiastically received. The enthusiasm makes me enthusiastic.[15]

EJ: But isn't this a form of dependence on the external eye and external energy. And isn't it risky? The enthusiasm is highly conditional. It's based in philosemitism and, as such, it can always turn ugly.

MS: For me, it's the continuation and the victory of what sprouted timidly in the '80s and I was momentarily a part of.

EJ: Yechiel Weizman, a doctoral student in Jewish history at the University of Haifa [today (2021) a professor of Holocaust studies at Bar-Ilan University], watched you dance in Wolnica Square in Kraków under a bas-relief depicting Jews falling at the feet of an angel wearing the crown of Casimir the Great. It's a work of Henryk Hochman's from 1907 titled *The Reception of the Jews in Poland in the Middle Ages*. This bas-relief was removed during the war, and it was restored by the city of Kraków in 1996.

MS: And he didn't like it that I danced?

EJ: He said you danced wonderfully. He couldn't take his eyes off you.

MS: He really didn't like it, I see. His irony though leads me to better understand what's going on here. Years ago, fundamental reading for me was *One-Dimensional Man* by Herbert Marcuse.[16] Reading both Marx and Freud, Marcuse developed the notion of *repressive desublimation* in order to understand the new stage in postwar capitalism. Classical capitalism required the repression of pleasure. In its new form, it's exactly the opposite. Libido is unleashed. But this eruption masks the real situation of actual, ongoing unfreedom. So that everything that I consider progress in the new Poland, you consider to be the next phase in the victory and domination of the majority over the minority, that is, the next phase of repression. But I—with one foot in Poland, the other in America—I see

---

15 See Eleanor Shapiro, *The Sound of Change: Performing "Jewishness" in Polish Small Towns*, doctoral dissertation, Graduate Theological Union, Berkeley, Cal., 2018.

16 Boston: Beacon Press, 1964.

this dance, for example, very simply and directly, unironically. It may be good to have an American passport in your pocket not just under communism …

EJ: I'd have to reread *One-Dimensional Man* because we read critical theory with Katarzyna Rosner all at once when in Poland there was a flood of Frankfurt School translations. I wasn't able to return to all of them later. But your description of things makes a lot of sense to me. To which I would add the current lack of support for all attempts at cultural critique and revision, that is, emancipatory thinking. Supporters of such things are mocked and marginalized here. Nowadays, even those who limit themselves to a non-critical approach are isolated. You don't have to address burning questions related to the present. It's enough to study Jewish history and culture for itself, without noticing the Christian public or empathizing with them, for attacks to ensue. Despite your praise for Yiddish scholarship in Poland, and rightly so, the Center for Yiddish Culture, led by a team of excellent scholars, is barely surviving. Their quarterly, *Cwiszn*, had to stop publication. The future of the bimonthly *Midrasz* is uncertain.[17] Look at ŻIH [Jewish Historical Institute] squashed by the MHŻP [Museum of the History of Polish Jews], including its access to public funding. And returning to what you call the interest in Jewish culture, how do you understand in this context the processes taking place in the public spaces of cities and towns? What I mean is the symbolic appropriation of sites – for example, with respect to Warsaw, in what Jacek Leociak has called *post-ghetto-space* [*miejsce-po-getcie*].[18]

MS: You know, I don't follow this close up. I'm not sure how to understand it. Actually, I was just at the Okopowa [Jewish] cemetery and saw that poster on the wall.

EJ: At the gate to the Jewish cemetery, there's a poster with the anchor sign of Fighting Poland advertising the film *The Warsaw Uprising* [about

---

17 *Midrasz* ceased publication in 2019.
18 See Elżbieta Janicka, *Festung Warschau*, preface by Bożena Keff (Warsaw: Wydawnictwo Krytyki Politycznej, 2011); Jacek Leociak, *Biografie ulic. O żydowskich ulicach Warszawy od narodzin po Zagładę* (Warsaw: Dom Spotkań z Historią, 2007).

the Polish uprising of 1944]. It's been hanging since April [2014], that is, for four months, something unheard of in the advertising business.[19]

MS: I did notice it but don't know what it means.

EJ: No poster ever hung on this wall. Neither communist, nor anti-communist. This is a cemetery wall, not advertising space.

MS: Fortunately, you don't have to see this inside the cemetery.

A poster advertising Jan Komasa's film *Powstanie warszawskie* [Warsaw Uprising] (2014): "First ever non-fiction war drama [...] see the true picture of the uprising." On the poster the logos of the Museum of the Warsaw Uprising, the distribution company Next Film, and the Polish Institute of Film Art. Entrance to the Jewish cemetery on Okopowa Street, Warsaw, July 1, 2014. Phot. Elżbieta Janicka.

---

19 EJ thanks Anna Zawadzka and Michał Wejroch for generously sharing their careful observations from the former Warsaw ghetto area.

EJ: Imagine the situation in reverse.

MS: An ad for a film about the ghetto uprising hanging on the wall of Powązki cemetery? Impossible! But maybe [Przemysław] Szpilman [caretaker of the Jewish cemetery since 2002] agreed?

EJ: Very possible. But could he not agree?

MS: Maybe he could. Though it would probably be badly understood. But again, what does this poster hinder? After all, it's hanging on the outside.

EJ: We have to start somewhere. Don't worry, we'll live to see the banner of Fighting Poland inside the cemetery.

MS: You exaggerate.

EJ: "The Gypsy will tell you the truth."[20]

---

20 Indeed, in 2018, with Polish state money, a giant Mausoleum of Jewish Fighters for the Independence of Poland was erected that dominates the cemetery. The original idea was formulated in 1938 by the commissar-president of the Jewish Community of Warsaw, who had been appointed by prewar Polish authorities known for their antisemitic policies.

Within the mass grave of thousands of anonymous Jewish victims of 1941–43, this *matseyve,* part of a memorial created by Hanna Szmalenberg and Władysław Klamerus in 1990, has had a small Polish flag with the symbol of the Polish uprising of 1944 added to it, thereby suggesting that the Jewish cause was considered by Poles intrinsic to the Polish cause. Jewish cemetery on Okopowa Street, July 30, 2015. Phot. Elżbieta Janicka.

"The passive death of the Jewish masses until now did not create any new values—it was useless" ("Last Act of a Great Tragedy," *Biuletyn Informacyjny* [main publication of the Polish Home Army], April 29, 1943 [two weeks after the start of the Warsaw Ghetto Uprising], nr. 17 [172], in Paweł Szapiro, ed., *Wojna żydowsko-niemiecka. Polska prasa konspiracyjna 1943–1944 o powstaniu w getcie warszawskim* [London: Aneks, 1992], p. 69). "[F]or all its exemplary democratic structure and its exalted national mission, or perhaps, more accurately, because of them, the 'underground state' was essentially for Poles only. [...] Its powerful bond to the community it defended was based on culture and blood, not citizenship, and this intimacy implied its mirroring of popular attitudes, including those about the Jews" (*Bondage to the Dead,* p. 37).

MS: When people go to a cemetery, what they care about is what's inside, not outside. I was there with my students; everyone saw that poster, and no one somehow said anything. But I didn't talk about it with Poles. It seems to me like an internal Polish matter. You know, there are four generations of Steinlaufs lying in this cemetery. And probably the same number of generations of Walds. I belong to this place; I belong to this ground. I love Warsaw and I belong to Warsaw. But Warsaw doesn't belong to me!

EJ: The minority corner is the place of the subtenant. This kind of poster-and-banner-hanging is an additional call to order. It makes the minority corner even stuffier and more claustrophobic.

MS: But I, as a Polish Jew—whatever that means today, but it means something for me—don't feel any claustrophobia. You'll answer that what's speaking out of me is a false, mystified consciousness, that I'm deceiving myself, that what's moving me is bad faith. But that would mean you're forgetting that I don't live in Poland, and I'm not bound to comply with your dominating discourse. That's why I feel free and can act accordingly. And my perspective is very different from yours. But I still can see that that poster which was hung on the wall of the cemetery was not put up with good intentions. If the intentions were good, it would not hang there. Perhaps I don't take it so seriously, but it's a subject to talk about with Szpilman. And with whoever hung that poster.

EJ: One clarification: I never for a moment assume that you think and act in bad faith. In that case, indeed, the matter would be simple and clear, and our talking would make no sense. It would be predictable and pointless.

I'd still like to return to the question of loyalty to one's own group— including groups acknowledged as one's own based on choice. Reading your book, I wonder whether in some key places you don't distance your- self from the murdered Jews. Maybe that's how we'll talk about them, because they didn't simply disappear, didn't stop existing on the strength of some vague dematerialization, but were murdered and now spread themselves around everywhere. Doesn't your narrative compromise their experience, in as much as they expressed this experience, and they did express it. You say yourself that that alleged silence of the victims wasn't what it later became suitable to believe.

MS: What you're concerned about is that I try to extend a hand to the Poles?

EJ: What I'm concerned about is the conditions under which you try to extend a hand to the Poles.

MS: You think I pay too high a price for it?

EJ: That's not saying enough. Perhaps Jews were denounced, you write, but Stefan "Grot" Rowecki was also denounced.[21]

MS: But wasn't he? Maybe Poles didn't suffer?

EJ: You set up a symmetry between phenomena that can't be compared. Or rather you reproduce and transmit a symmetry established—then and now—by the dominant Polish majority discourse.

MS: But I certainly don't negate what Gutman and Krakowski call "unequal victims."[22]

EJ: As a statement you don't negate it, agreed. But what results from suggesting the symmetry of fates and establishing a symmetry of discourses? What disappears from the field of vision is the asymmetry of fates, that first of all. Secondly, what disappears is the reactive and competitive nature of one of these discourses. Thirdly, from the perspective of the Polish audience, we approach the point at which facts become transformed into opinions.

MS: What are you saying here?

EJ: What I'm saying here is that the narrative—let's call it Gutman and Krakowski's—you *do* present. But as a result of inscribing it into a symmetry, you turn it into something non-binding, inconclusive. Some believe one thing, others something else. Its existence no longer makes it necessary to revise the assumptions of other narratives. You can put it into the minority corner, ascribe it to the subtenant, and the matter is taken care of. Seemingly there's a change taking place, but *de facto* everything remains the same.

MS: I recognized that you can't have everything. I had to decide on something.

---

21 Rowecki, commander of the Home Army, was denounced by Polish secret agents of the Gestapo, arrested by the Gestapo, and murdered in a Nazi concentration camp.

22 Gutman and Krakowski, *Unequal victims: Poles and Jews during World War Two.*

EJ: When emotional labor is only done by one side, it doesn't reflect well on the relations between the sides. The dominated side, of course, has to worry about the mood of the dominating one, because it's dependent on it. That's where the vaunted intuition of women and slaves comes from. That's the way it used to be. Now there's no longer a reason for it.

MS: But you forget that for me there's also another context and another audience, namely, American readers. Indeed, that's who the book was originally written for. You'd like to do everything at once, but here you have to go gradually.

EJ: Or the statement that demoralized Poles murdered demoralized Jews—in one breath? I'll pass over the fact that the murderers were not necessarily considered demoralized. After the war, whole villages defended them. In big factories, strikes erupted in defense of the perpetrators of the Kielce pogrom. And how do we know that the murdered Jews were demoralized? And if they were, what does that change?

MS: It helps explain the actions of Poles.

EJ: In general, or in their own understanding?

MS: Some have even applied this pattern to the Germans, but that's too much. It's also not easy to say that there were demoralized Poles. Yet Poles suffered terrible things.

EJ: But how about those demoralized Jews?

MS: Listen, in America no one knows anything, not about the Thirteen [group of powerful Warsaw ghetto gangsters] or Judenrats [Jewish councils] or the *Ordnungsdienst* [Jewish police].

EJ: As far as the Thirteen, the Judenrats, and the *Ordnungsdienst* are concerned, they were all murdered by the Germans. And let's not be surprised, studying the *Ordnungsdienst* and the Judenrats. Gutman, for instance, says something entirely different on this subject depending on whether he's involved in Zionist political correctness, or telling about his own experiences working in the Warsaw Judenrat and where—in the Provisioning Department![23] Intractable Raul Hilberg relented after reading Czerniaków's diary.[24] The Warsaw *Ordnungsdienst*—and not only the Warsaw one—doesn't especially resemble what we know about it from underground papers in the ghetto and from the dominant Polish narrative. Or take Perechodnik.[25] But let's leave this for a moment. Addressing the murder of the demoralized Jews you don't write anything about the Thirteen, Judenrats or *Ordnungsdienst*. The demoralized murder the demoralized. The equation in demoralization hides the lack of symmetry in their relations long before any war. Not to mention that in the third phase of the Holocaust one side had the power of life and death over the other. The status of these groups could not be more radically unequal.

MS: Here you're kind of convincing. Though I have to add that the third phase of the Holocaust is something new in the historiography.[26] We meet it only recently.

EJ: Let me read you something: "[T]he prevalence of informing, blackmail, plunder of various kinds, as well as the outright murder of Jews should not surprise us. City streets in the 'Aryan quarter' were the terrain of specialized gangs of blackmailers (the so-called *szmalcownicy*, from *shmalts*, Yiddish for grease), who scanned the physiognomy and posture of passersby seeking potential prey; in the forests, peasants, with or without German escort, hunted for Jews, whom they killed on the spot

---

23 Barbara Engelking and Israel Gutman, "Z profesorem Izraelem Gutmanem rozmawia Barbara Engelking," *Zagłada Żydów*, 2013 (9), p. 219.

24 *The Warsaw Diary of Adam Czerniakow: Prelude to Doom*, ed. by Raul Hilberg, Stanislaw Staron, and Josef Kermisz, trans. by Staron and the staff of Yad Vashem (New York: Stein and Day, 1979). Czerniakow was the chairman of the Warsaw Judenrat.

25 The 1996 English translation of Perechodnik's testimony was based on a twisted Polish version published by Ośrodek KARTA. See Calel Perechodnik, *Am I a Murderer? Testament of a Jewish Ghetto Policeman*, trans. and ed. by Frank Fox (Boulder, Colo.: Westview Press, 1996). The Polish publisher made up for the damage years later with a corrected version edited by David Engel that has not been translated into English thus far. See Calek Perechodnik, *Spowiedź [Confession]*, ed. by David Engel (Warsaw: Ośrodek KARTA, Dom Spotkań z Historią, 2011).

26 The term "third phase of the Holocaust" in recent Polish historiography refers to the hunt for escapees from death trains, ghettos, and camps. It is estimated that about 200,000 Jews were murdered in this way. See Engelking, *Such a Beautiful Sunny Day*; Grabowski, *Hunt for the Jews*; Engelking and Grabowski (eds.), *Dalej jest noc*.

or turned over to the Germans."[27] This was written in 1997 by Michael Steinlauf. Thus, we encounter this entirely new matter only today by virtue of and in the framework of "the ritual total surprise of the Polish intelligentsia."[28] If earlier studies were not undertaken in Poland by non-Jewish historians, they were undertaken by Jewish survivor-scholars in Poland and elsewhere. In Poland the matter was commonly known, nevertheless, and was present both in local consciousness and in high culture. Vast energy went into dissipating and counteracting this knowledge in many ways. But Wróblewski knew. And Halvorsen knew when he talked with Wróblewski. You yourself knew it when you were writing the book. Halvorsen knew it from the culture and the society. Wróblewski from his own experience. You, firsthand.

MS: You're thinking of what my mother heard on the roof? Yes, but I must remind you again that for one of the participants in that conversation there was, however, pity for the children dying in the ghetto.

EJ: "Yes, but." "However." Except that he somehow allowed himself to be silenced by the "rational" argument that Jewish children would turn into grown-up Jews.

MS: That's how my mother passed it on. The basic difference between us is that I don't take my thinking to its ultimate consequences as you're doing right now. Because you take it to the extreme. You're extremely extreme.

EJ: And you are extremely moderate.

MS: I wanted people to read this book. To read it in Poland and to read it in America.

EJ: And while writing the book, you thought about what people would say here and there, and not how things were and how the description of the subject should correspond to the subject of the description?

---

27 *Bondage to the Dead*, p. 40.
28 Janicka, "Mord rytualny," pp. 246–47.

MS: I didn't write the book for myself but for readers.

EJ: Murdering is the bottom of the bottom. The kind of bottom where things stop being complicated. Everyone's responsibility at this moment is solidarity with the murdered. I don't know … The responsibility is to not relativize that fact. Without respect to who belongs to what group and who they identify with.

MS: That's what Edelman used to say.[29] Agreed.

EJ: One doesn't need Edelman for that. I return to the question that's stuck in my throat. We spoke about responsibilities and loyalty. You said that one had responsibilities to everyone, but in relation to one's own group, specific ones. Later you said that the group you identify with is the murdered Jews. So that's how those specific responsibilities and specific loyalties turn out? I don't understand anything at this moment.

MS: It's all a question of balance. As usual, I get stuck between my specific place and the universal place. You can't just worry about your own dead even when they're most of the dead. But I wasn't sure even back then about those demoralized Jews which is why I put it in parentheses. Writing now, I'd write things differently, probably even leave out that reference. But in any case, in the situation that existed, it was a miracle that anyone at all saved Jews. A handful saved a handful. It's a miracle.

EJ: It's a miracle. But it's not an answer to my question.

MS: That construction might have been better thought out. But in the end, though, I don't excuse those who murdered Jews. How could I? But I have a question for you. Since so much of this is unacceptable to you, why are you putting so much time and energy into my book … and me as well?

EJ: First of all, this is a paradigmatic book. Humanities in Poland had performed the following maneuver: the traumatic paradigm, based on

---

29 Marek Edelman (1919–2009) was a member of the Jewish socialist Bund and one of the commanders of the Warsaw Ghetto Uprising. He remained in Poland after the war and was active in the Solidarity movement.

the experience of the victims of the Holocaust, a paradigm developed outside Poland, has been adopted as Polish and applied to Polish feelings about the Holocaust—exactly as you do. But the popularity of this notion isn't limited to the offices of academics of both sexes. Literary works, works of visual art, have followed it. Popular culture doesn't lag. "Polish trauma of the Holocaust" has entered the Polish lexicon. I'm not asserting that this wouldn't have happened without your contribution, except that your gesture has the value of legitimating the entire enterprise. Your book has given me no rest since it appeared in Polish. From 2010, I've actually read it in a circle, first dissecting every page into its basic elements, then putting them back together and observing how the discursive mechanism works, what it's made of and what purpose it serves. As though I were stepping into a laboratory, and into machines producing I don't know what—a happy fog conjuring well-being in people filled with the best intentions.[30] Except that it's a matter here of our life. Of what kind of world we want and are already making. It's a matter of what happened and of what we've done with it, are doing with it, and will do with it.

That's first of all. Secondly, at the cognitive, epistemic level I'm fascinated by how it's possible to produce such a narrative without any coercion, without being tangled up in the web of dependences, far from culture and society, that require such an act of homage as a daily matter. Thirdly, in the spring of 2014, long past midnight, as I'm hammering the last pins into the voodoo doll called the Polish experience of the Holocaust as collective trauma, the phone rings and it's the literary creation Michał Sztajnlauf, for that's how you introduced yourself. I didn't know which one of you was calling, the living Michael or the dead Michał. My heart stopped. As you are a literary historian you can understand. Then I felt an irresistible urge to find out who you are, a ravenous desire to talk. Fourth of all, it's awesome talking with you, we don't have to pretend about anything. We can talk about things that are usually not talked about in order not to antagonize people—even in academic circles. Fifth, you shared a lot of time and energy with me. You undertook the effort of

---

30 The reference is to Joanna Rajkowska's project "Oxygenator" (2007). This was a waterhole installed in Plac Grzybowski, equipped with a device for producing ozone fog. See Konrad Matyjaszek, "Przestrzeń pożydowska" [Post-Jewish space], *Studia Litteraria et Historica*, 2013 (2), pp. 130–147, https://doi.org/10.11649/slh.2013.006.

a conversation which is exhausting physically and psychologically. I too could ask why.

MS: Yes, I dug deep in this conversation. And despite the weakness of my Polish, which I never used in an analytical context and which you constantly have to correct. Particularly problematic when we get into polemics.

EJ: It's important for the text to maintain your literary standards, and in this area, you don't accept compromises. For nothing to be attributed to you that's contrary to your meaning, we carefully observe the principle of authorization. I'm concerned not to abuse your trust. And we work within the regimen of *slow science*. Without deadlines like "dinner is served."[31] We have as much time as we really need. And that includes the laborious process of you translating all this into English.

MS: Answering your question ... first of all, these conversations with you greatly help me in rethinking my book fifteen years after it appeared in Polish. It's an opportunity to make an accounting of what's changed in Polish historiography, what's changed in my thinking, and what's changed in myself. I'm asking myself how to synthesize these changes eventually in a new edition. And this connects to something more important about our conversations. Because we're talking here not only about my book, but about my life. Telling your own story is not simply organizing facts but searching for their meaning and perhaps even their purpose. It's important in that it's about trying to get to the heart of things. And I admit that these talks help me in shaping my own story, something I could accept as adequate. They help me make sense of my own story.

Warsaw, July 8 and 10, 2014

---

31 EJ: The reference is to Marek Piwowski's film *Rejs* (1970). The dialogue concerns the administration of justice in *ad hoc* mode and communicates the present-day realia of *fast science*. "Head Prosecutor: Good. Good. This means ... This means that I need time to work this matter out [...]. / Dumb-ass lecturer: Now to dinner ... That is, to dinner ... Take care of this, sir, please. But, colleague dear, we haven't any time. It's all eluding us" (scene 17).

Chapter 8

Moses ... Moyshe ... Michał ... Maryś ... Michel ... Michael ..., First Time Around

EJ: How did you know it was him?

MS: [Long silence.] I knew.

EJ: Do you remember the first time he appeared?

MS: It would be logical to say that he first appeared after my father's death, but it wasn't that way. When I think about it more deeply, it goes back to childhood. It was all brewing in me from the very beginning. After a while, I created for the subject—for him—a linear narrative, you know, a whole, with a beginning, a middle, and an end. You do that kind of thing when you want to exert some control over your experience. I arranged his life in order from birth to death, when he was two, maybe three years old.

I imagine that on that day, as usual, my father had been taken out for forced labor, while the mother sat with the child in the hideout. I don't know what happened there. I imagine that they're sitting in that hideout, probably with other Jews, crowded, hot, crazy with fear, the Aktion, the roundup, is raging, there's a blockade, they're close by, listening, and suddenly the child starts crying. And maybe they push the child out of the hideout, and it's still crying and calling, "Mamo." In Polish, it could only call in Polish. Did it happen that way? I don't know, I will never know, but this story is one possible version. My father later wanted nothing to do with this wife. He held her responsible for the child's death. That's what my mother told me. She, in any case, the wife, survived and left for Israel. And I believed, believed for a long time, that I carry inside me the dybbuk of that child. Hanna Krall wrote her story "The Dybbuk" based on talks we had in Warsaw, long ago, but she changed a lot, sometimes entirely unrecognizably. She turned me into a typical American with no sense of irony, which reminds me a bit, actually, of your attitude to me.[1]

EJ: Knowing me, it could have been much worse. And it's certainly worth talking about Hanna Krall's piece, but we should have the text in hand.

MS: Unfortunately, it only exists in English in a pretty abbreviated form. Then came Warlikowski's theater production *Dybuk* based on Anski's and Krall's versions.[2] I saw this production only as a video several years later.

EJ: Warlikowski's *Dybuk* met with a discerning reception throughout the world, but in the realm of Polish Jewish studies, it was treated in a superficial and simplistic manner. The idea of conceiving of Polish feelings about the Holocaust as a mass trauma is definitely not for me.[3] Told by others, your story lives its own life. It's hard to recover it. The phantasm

---

1   *Dowody na istnienie* (Poznań: Wydawnictwo a5, 1995), pp. 5–17. An abbreviated English version is in Antony Polonsky and Monika Adamczyk-Garbowska, eds., *Contemporary Jewish Writing in Poland* (Lincoln: University of Nebraska Press, 2001), pp. 312–16. See also Hanna Krall, *Różowe strusie pióra* (Warsaw: Świat Książki, 2009), pp. 92–93. In both texts, Michael Steinlauf appears as Adam S.

2   Premiere, Wrocław Film Studio, 2003, and subsequently performed throughout the world. See https://www.nytimes.com/2004/10/15/theater/reviews/two-tales-of-dybbuks-as-an-allegory-for-poland-and-judaism.html, and Michael C. Steinlauf, "Poland's Dybbuks: A response to the Warlikowski dialogues," *Polish Theatre Perspectives* 1 (2015), pp. 109–14.

3   On Polish "trauma" in the context of Warlikowski's staging of *Dybuk,* see Agnieszka Legutko, "Dybuk jako klucz do tożsamości," *Cwiszn* 1–2 (2014), pp. 32–42. See also her doctoral dissertation: *Possessed by the Other. Dybbuk Possession and Modern Jewish Identity in Twentieth-Century Jewish Literature and Beyond,* Columbia University, 2012.

or topos of the dybbuk currently finds itself in Poland under such solic-
itous care that a mouse can't slither through. Our interest could only
harm it. Let's return to your story with you, your father and Michał. Did
you really try to free yourself from him, and later—at the moment of his
parting—did you really try to stop him?

MS: Yes. That's how it really was. In Hanna Krall's telling there's a lot that's
off, but the Buddhist monk who's a Jew—exactly right. And it's right that
that monk found a way to me, or maybe to him, the dybbuk, or maybe
to him and me, to us both. And then tried to perform something like
an exorcism. "Go, go out to the light," he kept repeating. I felt something turn inside me and saw a shape something like a teddy bear but
very dark, start to move up and out of my gut. But suddenly I stopped
it all. Guess I decided to show him some solidarity—the dybbuk, that is.
Or better, some *rakhmunes*, which means something like compassion in
Yiddish. "Stay with me, don't go," I said. And he didn't need to be asked
twice and quickly slipped back into my body.

EJ: And maybe in this way you expressed solidarity with yourself?
Basically, a fine maneuver in a situation of choice. Because this was a situation of choice. No one had previously asked you for your opinion on the
furnishings of your interior. Except can you accept something that's so
radically unacceptable? To choose what had been imposed, to integrate
it, and in this way to gain an elementary integrity which you had been
deprived of precisely by the imposition and by what had been imposed.

MS: Maybe it can be described in this way. Especially because I'm a
rational person, someone who generally relies on the material world, so
I feel weird talking about dybbuks. But no, not about dybbuks. About
my dybbuk, about my brother, who is not alive but is real and bears—
bore?—my name, or rather I bear his. Once I found this intolerable. Now
I no longer battle with him so much about this name, though at the same
time I'm not sure if I've let go of the whole thing. But I don't have issues
with him, only with my father. My father never told me why he did it.
He never even told me that he did it. I lived with the belief that I was
named after my grandfather. And it is his name, though it's not after him
of course, but after my brother. What did he think? That is, my father. I'm

angry at him, furious. Why the hell did you give me the name of your murdered son? How can you do something like that to your own child? You don't do that! It's not all right! It isn't and it won't be. But despite everything, by now things have gotten easier. My insides are no longer tearing me apart. Because it was exactly as if someone extra was stuck in my guts, flailing around, and couldn't get out. Some insane deformed pregnancy. I say this, but I'm also listening to what I say, and recognize the words of a nut job and not some serious scholar.

EJ: What will people say?!

MS: What will people say—first of all, certainly!

EJ: You are justifiably angry because of the excavation of your person out of your person, the carving of your life out of your life. Because of the nullification of you as you. In relation to your father, right at the start you were placed—by your father—in an impossible position. You were not that child. You were you. Whatever you did, whoever you became, no matter how much you wanted to, you couldn't fulfill the expectation that tormented him. Your father inflicted unacceptable violence on you. He did it because his own suffering was too much for him, it incapacitated him, and he lost the ability to act in freedom. With your appearance— and your suffering—it all only became vaster. Your anger no longer has an addressee. Your parents are not alive.

MS: We're just returning from visiting them at the cemetery. And I'll tell you how surreal all of that Manhattan looks from there.

EJ: Talking to your parents may not necessarily have led to anything. Your father had agency, but we see that he lost control over the situation. Beyond that, we don't know what happened in that hideout then, in 1942, and if he was there. We don't know what he went through then and after. I don't justify him. I'm just trying to describe the state of affairs.

MS: I was completely alone with this story, that is, with this empti-ness, with this lack of history. Think about that dybbuk. It's not a tra-ditional dybbuk. It's the dybbuk of a child probably delivered to death. A child that screamed "Mamo!" which probably brought nothing to it

Michael Steinlauf by the grave of his parents, Reinfeld Family Circle, Beth David Cemetery, Elmont, New York, April 17, 2015. Hebrew inscription partly hidden under menorah: "Here rests Dvorah, daughter of R. Yeshayahu, d. Tevet 3, 5742." Below in English: "Doris, devoted wife, beloved mother, February 2, 1913-December 29, 1981." Hebrew inscription partly hidden under Star of David: "Here rests Zev, son of R. Moyshe, died Adar 5, 5727." Below in English: "William, beloved husband, devoted father, May 4, 1908-February 15, 1967." In the rear the grave of Helen (née Wilner) and Eric Steinlauf. In Hebrew: "Here rests Khaya Brokha, daughter of R. Yankev Avner"; "Here rests Arye Yehuda Leyb, son of R. Moyshe." Phot. Elżbieta Janicka.

Michael Steinlauf, Beth David Cemetery, Elmont, New York, April 17, 2015. Phot. Elżbieta Janicka.

but a German. A child—judging by the photographs—that didn't look so Jewish [*podobny do Żyda*] but got a bullet in its head. Or who had a German smash its head against a wall, or against the stairs, or against something else.

EJ: You left out one possibility, or most likely, probability—that his mother smothered him in the hideout to end his crying.

MS: [Long silence.] You may be right … And that may explain why my father wanted nothing to do with her after the war. He returns to the ghetto after a day of digging ditches or whatever and finds … horror.[4]

EJ: Dybbuks aren't that much my field of expertise. But isn't it the case that a classic dybbuk when it lived broke some precept or prohibition? And its fate is then used to discipline the community.

---

4   On the fate of young children in hideouts, EJ presents the testimony of Szymon Datner years after the war. He was testifying, both as witness and expert, in a West German court in the trial of the German murderers in the Białystok ghetto. During the liquidation of the ghetto, he was taken out daily to work and returned in the evening. His family spent this time in a hideout below an apartment in which there were some others. One day, upon returning, Datner found two corpses. One was of four-year-old Basia, the daughter of a teacher of Latin, a colleague of Datner's from the Hebrew gymnasium where they taught before the war. Datner testified as follows: "The one who smothered the child was a professor of mathematics named Lubelski. And if this Lubelski stood before this court, before me, I would not call him a murderer, though he killed, but the situation was such that the child had been given luminal [a sleeping pill] […]—this luminal was of war-time quality, it was no good, and at the moment when the Germans came in, the child woke up, started crying, and this crying could have betrayed everyone […]. So Professor Lubelski, to keep the Germans upstairs from hearing the crying, wanted to quiet her. He didn't want to murder her; it turned out that he apparently squeezed too hard." Datner also describes the struggles with the dead child's body: "I didn't have a shovel, I had to use the small shovel from the oven. It was winter. […] I dug a small little grave. And the sound of the shovel woke me to terror, especially since behind me stood the mother with this child. And she even asked me at the last moment: 'The gentleman seems to know, maybe she's still alive.' And this was a child that was already stiff. I buried her, covered her with snow. After the German action, we buried her in the cemetery. [Sworn testimony of Dr. Szymon Datner in Bielefeld in the criminal trial of Wilhelm Altenloh and others, syg. 5 Ks 1/65, 2 May 1966, nr 6341, tape nr. 18, p. 1, in Katrin Stoll, "O walce i zagładzie białostockiego getta" in Szymon Datner, *Walka i zagłada białostockiego getta* (Warsaw: ŻIH, 2014), p. 105].

MS: Precisely. And here we're talking about a two-year-old child! So, what are we talking about? Anski redid the dybbuk tale as something sweet. His dybbuk was a romantic lover. He lacks the horrible and the violent, which are standard in the traditional stories. Because a real dybbuk is terrifying. And my dybbuk is terrifying. One of my ex-students wrote a study of the roots of the phenomenon dating back to the sixteenth century. Various dybbuks appear in various texts down to the twentieth century. They make themselves known in various situations and are carefully observed. Contemporary rabbis were kept busy doing exorcisms. One of the dybbuks, I recall, was asked why he became a dybbuk after his death. He replied that it was because he slept with boys.

EJ: So that's clear. He transgressed a fundamental classification lying at the heart of the social order.

MS: *Yeshive bokher.* Yeshiva boy. He transgressed. We know what to think of that classification, but at least he transgressed something, did something. But little Moyshe, little Michał Steinlauf, what did he transgress, what did he do?

EJ: He transgressed another classification.

MS: A German one?

EJ: If only it were just German. A Christian one.

MS: With his very existence. This is not to be conceived or accepted. Nor how our father disposed of us.

EJ: So here the thing must lie with your father. At the very root of your existence, he implanted the violence and the suffering he had experienced, and which are beyond human endurance. You could only seek help with your mother, who was herself filled with grief and other similar abysses. Survivors are rarely survivors. And now go and lift that off your soul.

MS: I worked it out to the extent that I decided to try to accept the load and somehow overpower it with compassion. I told him to stay. But I don't know if I'm dealing so well with the result.

EJ: Was it better than if you'd sent him away then?

MS: Maybe yes, maybe no. Impossible to say.

EJ: Anski made of the dybbuk and the cultural convention of possession a medium for revolt against an oppressive social order. It's a bit too bad that his emancipatory heroine doesn't make it out alive from this emancipation. But finally, it's only a trifle. We're used to this. It's so feminine. It adds to her charm. On the other hand, I can't believe that there exists an attempt—supposedly following in Anski's steps—to redo post-Holocaust dybbuks as a source of positive energy, therapeutic strength, an instrument for conquering anything. Not only in America. Also in Poland.[5] That's not the case with you though.

Do we end here, or do we leave some scrap of redemptive narrative for the finale?

MS: You know, I'm starting to look towards old age.

EJ: I'm afraid that it may not be so good even then.

MS: So maybe, let's say that regardless of everything—it's better that he stayed.

New York, April 17, 2015

---

5   On subsequent stagings and other dybbuk sightings, see Mieczysław Abramowicz, Jan Ciechowicz and Katarzyna Kręglewska, eds., *Dybuk. Na pograniczu dwóch światów* (Gdańsk: Wydawnictwo Uniwersytetu Gdańskiego, 2017).

Chapter 9

Moses ... Moyshe ... Michał ... Maryś ... Michel ... Michael ..., Second Time Around

EJ: Tomorrow will be a year from our first conversation. July again, heat wave, Warsaw. Barefoot again.

MS: On Polish soil.

EJ: Thanks for reminding me. I might have forgotten. The issue of the Polishness of the soil, this soil, we'll register in our discrepancy protocol. This is, after all, Saska Kępa [Saxon Island] and Łotewska [Latvian] Street. Before, we were at Litewska [Lithuanian] Street. Also nice. So, we're going barefoot a year later on the other side of the Vistula, with a view of the Palace of Culture. Everywhere the smell of a wild living river. We're talking over a pile of photographs and documents that you extracted from a box in your home in Philadelphia. How did you come by them?

MS: My mother's university papers come from the archives of the University of Warsaw. The university suffered a direct hit during the war. A lot of the archives burned. Not my mother's. They survived by accident, like my mother. I first saw them in 1983. Xeroxes at the time were worth their weight in gold. You needed permission for every copy. I was afraid to admit to the archivist why I wanted copies of these documents. Finally, I told her that Dwojra Wald was my mother. She snapped at me, displeased I hadn't told her at once. See how beautifully they xeroxed everything for me. Nowadays this xerox is itself a historic document. And see how much there is here. Birth certificate, 14 February 1911, father Szaja Wald, mother Zysła Wajchenberg. "This certificate of birth was recorded in the annals of the Mosaic faith in the 7th state police headquarters of the capital city of Warsaw." They had separate forms for the Mosaic faith. Nowadays it wouldn't be worth it to print separate ones. Then a diploma from Fanny Posnerowa's Women's Gymnasium in Warsaw on Twarda 27. What's there now?

EJ: The U.N. traffic circle and subway station. The intersection of John Paul II Street, Świętokrzyska and Prosta. Buses. Trolleys. In the resume of Dwojra Waldówna, Grzybowska 17, apt. 26—attached to the 1928 application to the Humanities Division of the University of Warsaw, it says Posnerowa's was a humanities gymnasium.

MS: This is what her graduation exams show she studied: religion (it's not mentioned which), Polish language, German language, history and study of contemporary Poland, mathematics. Other subjects: Latin language, physics and chemistry, preparatory philosophy, drawing, anatomy. Fives [A's] in religion and preparatory philosophy, a three [C] in German, fours [B's] in all the rest. See, as I said. No Jewish history, no Hebrew, of course no Yiddish.

EJ: But here's a document entitled "Statistical Form" which Dwojra Waldówna—parents' place of residence Nalewki 23, apt. 134—completed in 1933–34. Citizenship Polish. Mosaic faith. Native language Yiddish.

MS: This was for the official statistics, on the basis of which the state was supposed to fulfill its responsibilities to minorities as part of the Minority Treaty of the Treaty of Versailles. Those responsibilities were generally ignored.

EJ: In 1934, Poland unilaterally renounced the Minority Treaty.

MS: It kept getting worse, so that Jewish newspapers and organizations called for Jews to list Yiddish as their mother tongue as a political gesture. Therefore the disparity between the official statistics and actual Jewish language use. Ezra Mendelsohn writes about this.[1] This was a statement about identity. In this way, my mother showed her solidarity with other Jews. She certainly didn't know Yiddish. Linguistically she was completely assimilated, but she would never ever call herself a Pole. She would have defined herself as a Polish Jew, as would the great majority of the Jews in Poland.

EJ: Why the discrepancy between the dates on her birth certificate and on her grave? In her Polish papers it says 1911, on her grave it's 1913.

MS: My mother once told me that her parents wanted her admitted to school earlier than her actual date of birth would have allowed. So they put 1911 in her papers though the real year of her birth was 1913. I don't know if that's true, but it's the only thing I ever heard on the subject.

EJ: And how about the discrepancy between your mother's address and her parents'?

MS: I have no idea. It's hard to imagine her parents would allow their youngest child, the apple of their eye, out of their home.

EJ: Because this played a role in the later fate of the Wald family. Nalewki was in the large ghetto, Grzybowska in the small one.

---

1   A question about mother tongue appeared in the Polish census of 1931. In a situation in which Yiddish, it was judged, was in crisis if not in decline: "All in all, 79.9 percent of Polish Jewry declared Yiddish to be its mother tongue, and 7.8 percent obeyed the command of the Zionist movement and declared (falsely) its mother tongue to be Hebrew. Those who described themselves as Polish-speaking from childhood obviously belonged to the acculturated segment of the Polish Jewish community. [...] It may be noted that there is no absolute correlation between the choice of national affiliation and mother tongue. [...] The language a Polish Jew might speak in his home, along with the nationality he might wish to indicate on a census form, certainly tells us something about his degree of acculturation and assimilation. But his answers do not enable us to predict with total accuracy his attitude toward his Jewishness and toward the dilemma of being a Jew in Poland" (*The Jews of East Central Europe Between the World Wars*, pp. 30–32).

MS: But when war broke out, she was living in the countryside. And she probably never again lived officially in Warsaw. Her university papers show that she was an excellent student. And in her tuition records, taken from the bursar's office, we have the names of her professors: Marceli Handelsman, Stanisław Arnold, Jan Kochanowski, Tadeusz Kotarbiński, Władysław Tatarkiewicz, Stefan Czarnowski, Oskar Sosnowski, Oskar Halecki, Stefan Baley, Władysław Sterling, Hanna Pohoska. These were well-known academics, some were famous. I mention them all as a way of remembering a lost world. She wrote her master's thesis under Arnold: "The Situation of Peasants in the Economies of Brwillno and Borowe in the Years 1815–1830 (in the province of Mazovia)." Admitted to studies, 24 October 1928, Master of Philosophy diploma awarded 30 June 1933. In America she tried, but she couldn't put this to use in any way. Besides, my father didn't want her to work. She was his queen and he wanted her to remain that way. So she watched over me and read books.

EJ: What did your father do here?

MS: He set up his own one-man business. He got to be on good terms with the foremen in the clothing factories who would order things from him like needles and belting for the sewing machines as well as spot remover. After a while, he started to specialize in this. He began with something with a felt top that he called Tip-Z-Top. Then he went on to an aerosol can. I've got this late version, Quick Spot Remover, standing on a shelf in my bedroom. If he hadn't died so young, he would have made a bit of money and retired to Florida like the others.

EJ: In the marriage certificate, your mom is Dorota. In America she decided on Doris. Why, since Dwojra is Deborah?

MS: In the 1950s in America, there were few Deborahs, but the name Doris was common. The actress and singer Doris Day was very popular then. Doris was a good choice.

EJ: And why did your father take the name William?

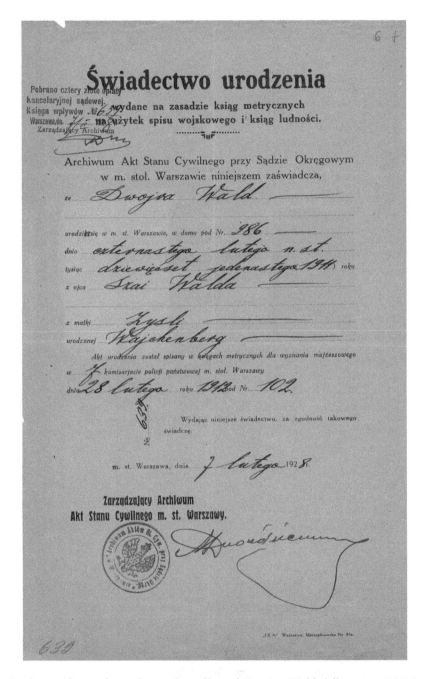

Birth certificate, from the student files of Dwojra Wald (album nr. 29425, syg. RP 29425). Copyright Archives of the University of Warsaw.

Matura [Secondary school diploma, front followed by back], document from the student files of Dwojra Wald (album nr. 29425, syg. RP 29425). Copyright Archives of the University of Warsaw.

Poza tem uzyskał a___ ostatnie oceny roczne w klasach VI — VIII
(lub odpowiednie oceny na egzaminie wstępnym do wymienionego gimnazjum)
z przedmiotów następujących:

z jęz. łacińskiego *dobrą*   ze śpiewu i muzyki _____

z fizyki wraz z chemją *dobrą*   z ćwiczeń cielesnych _____

z propedeutyki filozofji *bardzo dobrą*   z anatomji *dobrą*

z rysunku *dobrą*   z _____

Państwowa Komisja Egzaminacyjna uznała _____

___WALD DWOJRĘ___ za dojrzał ą do studjów
wyższych i wydaje___jej___ niniejsze świadectwo.

___Warszawa___ dnia 2 czerwca roku 1928

Nr. 13/86

PRZEWODNICZĄCY
PAŃSTWOWEJ KOMISJI EGZAMINACYJNEJ

CZŁONKOWIE
PAŃSTWOWEJ KOMISJI EGZAMINACYJNEJ

University registration, document from the student files of Dwojra Wald (album nr. 29425, syg. RP 29425). Copyright Archives of the University of Warsaw.

Statistical form, document from the student files of Dwojra Wald (album nr. 29425, syg. RP 29425). Copyright Archives of the University of Warsaw.

UNIWERSYTET WARSZAWSKI

WYDZIAŁ HUMANISTYCZNY

Nr 1224/2684/33.

DYPLOM MAGISTRA FILOZOFJI

PANI DWOJRA WALD

URODZONA DNIA 14 LUTEGO 1911 ROKU W WARSZAWIE

odbyła przepisane studja w Uniwersytecie Warszawskim na Wydziale Humanistycznym w zakresie h i s t o r j i i zdala następujące egzaminy:

z zasad metody badań historycznych, podstawowych wiadomości z nauk pomocniczych oraz źródeł historycznych w zakresie historji Polski z wynikiem bardzo dobrym

z dziejów starożytnych . . . . z wynikiem bardzo dobrym

z dziejów średniowiecznych (polskich i powszechnych) . . . . z wynikiem bardzo dobrym

z dziejów nowożytnych i nowoczesnych (polskich i powszechnych) . . . . z wynikiem dostatecznym

z głównych zasad nauk filozoficznych . . . . z wynikiem bardzo dobrym

z pogłębionej znajomości dziejów społecznych polskich w latach 1815 — 1830 . . . . . z wynikiem dostatecznym

Sig. F. 2.
Drukarnia Państwowa Nr 09640. 6.IV.34.

Master of Philosophy diploma [front followed by back], with the signatures of Rector Józef Ujejski; Dean of the Humanities Division, Marceli Handelsman; Chair of the Examining Committee, Stanisław Szober; document from the student files of Dwojra Wald (album nr. 29425, syg. RP 29425). Copyright Archives of the University of Warsaw.

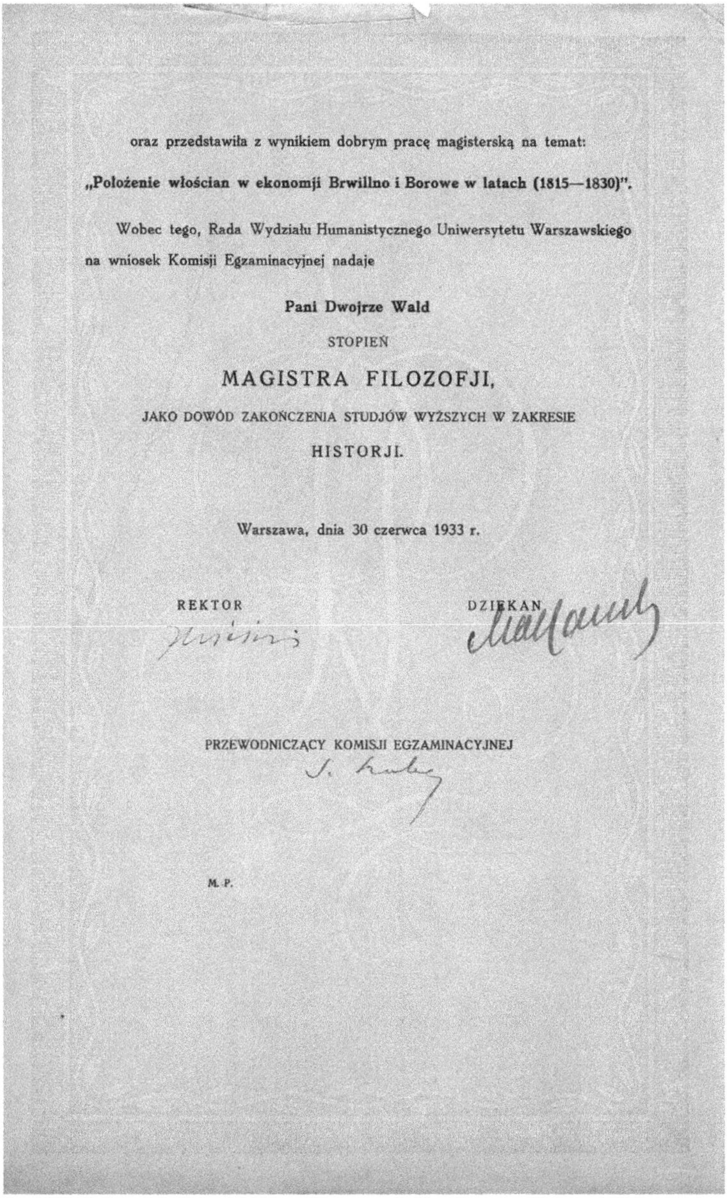

oraz przedstawiła z wynikiem dobrym pracę magisterską na temat:

„Położenie włościan w ekonomji Brwillno i Borowe w latach (1815—1830)".

Wobec tego, Rada Wydziału Humanistycznego Uniwersytetu Warszawskiego na wniosek Komisji Egzaminacyjnej nadaje

Pani Dwojrze Wald

STOPIEŃ

MAGISTRA FILOZOFJI,

JAKO DOWÓD ZAKOŃCZENIA STUDJÓW WYŻSZYCH W ZAKRESIE

HISTORJI.

Warszawa, dnia 30 czerwca 1933 r.

REKTOR   DZIEKAN

PRZEWODNICZĄCY KOMISJI EGZAMINACYJNEJ

M.P.

Dwojra Wald, c. 1944. Copyright Michael Steinlauf.

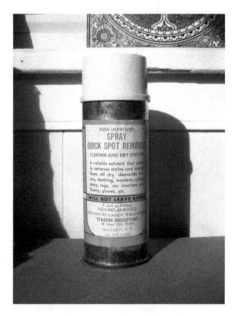

Quick Spot Remover. Phot. Elżbieta Janicka.

MS: William is Wolf of course. He wanted his name to be as American as possible, so he gave himself the middle name Robert. He called the business Stason Industries from Steinlauf and son. For correspondence in New York, he used William R. Steinlauf Co., but for letters sent out of New York, "to the provinces," he made up stationery with Stason Industries on it.

EJ: What name or word did you parents use to refer to you?

MS: Michael. I remember my mother calling "My-kool!" And when I was little, it was Misiu [*Mee-shu*]. My memory is of her saying this in a very soft voice.

EJ: And what did they call each other?

MS: Władek and Dorka. They frequently held hands. Even years after their marriage. My father used to repeat like a mantra that the only good years in his life were those he spent with my mother.

EJ: Did they ever talk about the Rosenbergs?

MS: I was very little. I remember them whispering the name. Here were "Jewish communist traitors" in the McCarthy era and they had just arrived in America. Imagine.

EJ: How do you remember your bar mitzvah?

MS: The bar mitzvah was at the Hebrew Alliance of Brighton Beach. With this goal in mind my parents sent me to what was known as a Hebrew school. I went only a couple of times. The teacher was a young hasid who would smack kids on the knuckles with a ruler. Pretty old-school.

EJ: I know! He would whack you and then you'd have to write the letters correctly. My father was the beneficiary of such methods before the war in France in a totally secular school where the kids were whacked just the same to instill pride for the heritage of revolution.

MS: As a result of this introduction to Jewish things, later at Brandeis I had to learn everything from scratch. Including the alphabet. I didn't even know the sequence of letters, so I couldn't use a Hebrew diction-ary. After the business with the hasid, my parents found an elderly gentleman who wore an antiquated cantor's yarmulka. He was called Mr. Braun. And Mr. Braun came to our home. Still, by today's stand-ards, this was not much in the way of learning. My sons' bar mitzvahs were serious events. They were responsible for running the entire ser-vice. They had to know what came after what. Each chanted his *parsha* [weekly Torah portion] directly from the Torah scroll. Then they had to chant the *haftorah* [associated biblical text] to a different tune. I had to learn only the *haftorah*. I had no idea about anything else. But not only me. This was the 50's. No one cared much about tradition, not to mention religion. What was important was the evening reception for a hundred-fifty people.

EJ: A sign of status?

MS: Status and belonging, because everyone did it. And my bar mitzvah, I think, was somewhat fancier than usual in Brighton Beach. For my par-ents it must have been a terrible expense. They must have been saving up for years. And everything turned out perfectly. Dressed-up guests, lots of food, live music and dancing, and a photographer for the whole day. And then the album.

EJ: You mean that huge leather-bound volume. We can hardly lift it. No question that this object was thought of as eternal. And similarly, the people in the photographs are showing that they made it, that they're alive and like everyone else—a memento for all time. This album was probably the most important thing.

MS: And that's probably why the only thing I had to write and prepare for the bar mitzvah in English was a speech to the guests gathered in the synagogue.

EJ: A speech with an exegesis of the *parsha*?

MS: What kind of exegesis?! Today the speech has to be about the *parsha*. Today there are even speeches by parents, often separate speeches by the mother and the father. None of this existed back then,

EJ: But you must have chanted *Sh'ma Yisrael*.[2]

MS: I must have but I don't remember. I would have had no idea what it meant. But what got to me wasn't the speech but something entirely different. Several years before, I had started playing the accordion. My parents got me a beautiful grey ivory one. Before my bar mitzvah it occurred to my father for me to perform as a soloist with my music teacher's band. And to show off my talent I would play nothing less than "Flight of the Bumble Bee." Can you imagine? I couldn't sleep because of that Rimsky-Korsakov, and at the bar mitzvah I was too nervous to touch any of the delicious food heaped up on the main table. I survived somehow, but soon after I put away the accordion. Years later I loaned it to a student rock group at Columbia and it was stolen from the back of their pick-up truck.

EJ: In other words, your initiation into Judaism was a terrible hassle.

MS: It sure was ... But to prepare me for my speech in English there was Glikson. That's how they referred to him. Simply Glikson. Before the war he was a well-known actor in the Yiddish theater, a leading member of the Yung-teater company directed by Michał Weichert.[3] This was an avantgarde troupe which the young Jewish intelligentsia streamed in to see. And knowledgeable Polish theater people would come and marvel. Glikson had a really beautiful wife. It was hard for me to concentrate around her. Tsipora—and in Polish, Pojcia [Poytsha]. They were a strange pair, because Glikson was very short, dwarfish. But he was a fantastic dancer and always filled with amazing energy.

EJ: On the Museum of Jewish Heritage page, I found this photograph. Have a look.

---

2   "Hear, O Israel, the Lord is our God, the Lord is One," essential Jewish prayer.
3   *YIVO Encyclopedia* 2: 2104-05; https://yivoencyclopedia.org/article.aspx/Yung-teater

Left to right: Josef Glikson (1899–1992), Zipporah Faynzilber-Glikson (1914–2008), David Minster. Tashkent, c. 1945. Courtesy of Museum of Jewish Heritage.

MS: It's them! Pojcia! Glikson! See for yourself. Didn't I tell you? The photograph was taken in Uzbekistan. In Tashkent.

EJ: Glikson in glasses and a shirt with folk-style embroidery.

MS: Look, here's a certificate from the Union of Polish Patriots in the Soviet Union that this very Pojcia worked as an artist in the artistic ensemble in Tashkent until May 1, 1946, "conscientiously discharging her duties." Stamped. Signatures. She didn't leave with the Anders army.[4] And to think that years later I wrote about Pojcia, who just before the war played Miranda in Shakespeare's *Tempest*.[5] That *Tempest* in Yiddish,

---

4   In March 1942, the Soviet Union permitted the formation of an army composed primarily of Polish ex-POW's and civilian deportees. It was popularly known by the name of its commander, Władysław Anders. The army, which had an antisemitic reputation, returned to fight in Europe by way of Iran and Palestine.

5   *YIVO Encyclopedia* 2: 1866; https://yivoencyclopedia.org/article.aspx/Theater/Yiddish_Theater

translated by the poet Arn Tsaytlin, was an important artistic event but also a symbolic one. It was an attempt to demonstrate Polish-Jewish solidarity on the eve of war. The best-known left-wing Polish theater people collaborated in the production. It was directed by Leon Schiller, scenography by Władysław Daszewski and choreography by Tacjanna Wysocka. Pojcia was eighteen years old at the time. And Prospero was played by none other than Avrom Morewski, who, as the Rebbe of Miropol, had exorcised the dybbuk in the 1920 premiere of Anski's play!

EJ: And here's a poster from their postwar appearance in Warsaw. Provincial Jewish Committee in Warsaw. Division of Culture. "Prague Revue." Literary-Artistic Morning Production. Artistic portion starring Cypora Fajnzylber and Josef Glikson. October 20, 1946. Three months after the Kielce pogrom, this poster announces that Jewish life in Poland exists and continues. It would still take many years of hard work by your traumatized Polish witnesses of the Holocaust to finally liquidate this life.

Michael Steinlauf's bar mitzvah, January 1960. Left to right: Josef Glikson, Pojcia Glikson, Michael Steinlauf. Copyright Michael Steinlauf.

MS: More things intersect here. Because in that photograph from Tashkent, besides the Gliksons, there's David Minster. Also an actor. And part of our family history. After my father's death—as a result of my father's death—my mother tried to run the business. The idea was that she would sit at the little desk in the warehouse and someone else would work outside. So Glikson suggested Minster. They had obviously stayed in touch for all these years. So Minster tried, but nothing came of it. Neither of them—neither he nor my mother—had the slightest talent for business. This wasn't what they were meant for. And so, the handsome performer in that photograph I remember as the harried aging salesman dragging himself into the office off the steaming New York streets and falling into a chair. It didn't work out—for either of them—and my mother sold the business soon after for a pittance.

EJ: All this was in 1967, which happens to coincide with the catastrophe of the Yiddish theater in Poland. The Yiddish theaters in Łódź and Wrocław had closed their doors earlier, but in Warsaw there was still the legendary State Yiddish Theater of Ida Kaminska,[6] to a great extent a traveling theater because it still had places to travel to. Except that precisely in June of that year at the Congress of Trade Unions, [Władysław] Gomułka's antisemitic speech was transmitted by radio and television. To Ida Kaminska it felt as though she was listening to Nazi speeches of the 1930's. Soon after came March and the rest of 1968,[7] so she abandoned this glamorous scene—along with the State Yiddish Theater building that was being built for her company—and left Poland. Her postwar public dissolved a bit more with each new antisemitic eruption. Except that never before had the official instigators of such attacks been the state and the ruling party. Had Ida Kaminska remained in Poland at that time, she would have functioned as a fig leaf for this state and party antisemitism, and this she didn't want. In New York she tried to open a Yiddish theater. In vain.

MS: Correct. And if it was hard for Ida Kaminska in New York, by what miracle should it have been easy for Minster?

EJ: Say something more about your home.

---

6   *YIVO Encyclopedia* 2: 1420; https://yivoencyclopedia.org/article.aspx/Polish_State_Yiddish_Theater

7   The antisemitic campaign launched by the government resulted in the emigration of some 20,000 Jews.

MS: In our little apartment, there was only one bedroom. Which my parents, naturally, gave to me. They themselves slept in the living room on something called a Murphy bed which came down from a special alcove at night and went back up vertically during the day. I don't think they have them anymore. What else? Maybe because in the Wald home there was a maid, or maybe for some other reason, my mother was not much of a housewife. Certainly, occasionally she made sweet and sour stuffed cabbage with raisins and lemons, which I loved, but besides this, in general, not much. On holidays she also made an apple tart, apples on top, crust on the bottom, but the whole thing was usually pretty dry. I wasn't crazy about that tart. She also baked apples. Holidays— I'm thinking of Passover—weren't anything fancy. The first seder was generally at our house, just the three of us. But at the second seder at Helen and Eric's house in Queens there were lots of people. There was us. There was Myra's husband Ed's parents, Belgian Jews. There was Henryk Wilner, Helen's brother who she'd saved along with Eric and Myra. Henryk liked to eat and drink. He had the reputation that in Poland he used to drink with the Poles. He didn't enjoy a lot of respect in the family, but he couldn't have cared less. Eventually he married and his wife Ethel would come to the seders too. And Eric, the ex-yeshiva boy, would hum *nigunim* after the huge meal, then join Henry on the couch for a nap.

My mother, with her culture, was always a bit apart. And that's the way she remained. Delicate and sensitive. From another world, not like her neighbors on Church Avenue, which is where she moved after her third husband died. When she died, one of her neighbors said: "Your mother was a lady."

My father regularly had nightmares. I would hear him groaning sometimes when I woke up at night. Once, I remember, he screamed terribly. Shrieked. As though you were ripping his skin off. I could have been eleven, twelve years old. I didn't dare ask him about it. I always knew he'd been in the ghetto and that this was about that. And that was all.

EJ: And your father's death?

MS: I wasn't living at home then, but in upper Manhattan near Columbia. I was halfway through my last year of study. February. My father had a major heart attack. I went to see him at the hospital in Brooklyn. He was

Seder at Aunt Helen's, mid-1970's. Left to right: David Fischer, his mother Myra Fischer [née Steinlauf], Pojcia Glikson, Josef Glikson, Ethel Wilner, Helen Steinlauf, Eric Steinlauf, Ed Fischer's father, Henryk Wilner, Ed Fischer's mother, Doris Steinlauf, her husband Martin Kwintner.

in bad shape. He held out his hand and I took it. We held hands for a bit. Then he threw up into a basin and fell back onto his pillow. Next day my mother called to tell me to come home. My father had died. It was four days before my twentieth birthday.

After my mother's call I walked to the subway, I remember. I looked west, to Riverside Park, the Hudson River. It was beautiful over there. I realized that things would never be the same, that my life was changing in fundamental and irreversible ways.

The funeral came quickly, as is the Jewish custom. There was a rabbi. I must have said *kaddish*. But what I really remember is that after they'd lowered the coffin, my mother started to scream "Władek! What have you done!? How could you? How could you leave me?" And then, "I won't allow it!" She had to be restrained from throwing herself on the coffin. She later told me that when we got home, I started banging my head against the wall. This I don't remember.

EJ: How did you get the photographs of your father's first family?

MS: A few years after Helen, my uncle Eric's wife, died, Myra sent them to me. Those from before the war we had at home. But there were ones from the ghetto that I'd never seen. I have no idea how Helen and Eric got them. While they were alive, they never showed them to me. I don't know if my mother ever saw them. My uncle died in 1989, my aunt in 2001. I received the photographs sometime later, and of course mislaid them soon after. They turned up eventually, but in the meantime, in 2008, Myra sent me new copies.

EJ: "Dear Mike," Myra writes in the first letter, "Enjoy the photographs, Stay well, love."

MS: "Enjoy?" Hard to believe. On the other hand, each time Myra carefully describes who is who. She knows it all, remembers, but she's compartmentalized it, put it in a separate mental drawer.

This is the earliest photograph I have of my father, sitting over a chessboard with his cousins, that is, sons of my grandfather's brother. The brothers—Murray (with the bangs) and Harry—left Poland for America early on and shortened their name to Stein.

Wolf Sztajnlauf with cousins, Poland, early 1920's. Left to right: Wolf, Murray Stein, Harry Stein. Copyright Michael Steinlauf.

And here's my father in the resort town of Otwock [Otvotsk] probably. In a suit and tie, elegant, snazzy. You pointed out that he's reading *Nasz Przegląd*.[8] This was also doubtless a family in which the parents read *Haynt*[9] and the children *Nasz Przegląd*. Like the Walds. And probably like the rest of their friends. Although unlike the Walds, the children could also have handled *Haynt*. The picture would make a good advertisement for *Nasz Przegląd*. My father had style. He stood out, knew how to be noticed.

Wolf Sztajnlauf reading *Nasz Przegląd*, 1930s. Copyright Michael Steinlauf.

---

8   *Nasz Przegląd* [Our review] appeared throughout most of the interwar period. It was a large-circulation Jewish daily in the Polish language. Among other things, it popularized Yiddish as well as modern Hebrew literature and published works in Polish translation. In the years 1926–39, inspired by the educator Janusz Korczak, it published a free Friday supplement entitled *Mały Przegląd* [Little review] created by and intended for children. On this and other Polish-language Jewish newspapers, see Michael Steinlauf, "The Polish Jewish Daily Press," *Polin: A Journal of Polish-Jewish Studies*, 2 (1987), pp. 219–45, reprinted in Antony Polonsky, ed., *From Shtetl to Socialism: Studies from Polin* (London: Littman Library, 1993), pp. 332–58.

9   *Haynt* [Today], one of two major Yiddish dailies, Zionist-oriented and read especially by the middle class, appeared throughout 1908–1939.

Runia Sztajnlauf, sister of Wolf and Eric, Otwock, 1920. Copyright Michael Steinlauf.

Runia and Wolf, Otwock, 1930s. Copyright Michael Steinlauf.

And this is my father's only sister, Runia. Otwock, 1920

EJ: "At resort," Myra writes.

MS: And here is almost the entire family. In the first row, my grandfather Moyshe, my father's father, a Gerer hasid, no doubt about it. But for a traditional Jew, he had modern impulses. He traveled to Palestine, bought and sold land there. He named Eric Arye Leyb after the rebbe, but gave my father the non-traditional name Zev. Next to him is his wife, my grandmother Nechuma. Next to her is either her sister or Runia's mother-in-law, her husband Bolek's mother. Behind her, Bolek. Behind Nechuma, Runia. Behind my grandfather, my uncle Eric. My grandfather died in 1930, so this is in the '20s. Runia and Bolek's children weren't born yet. My father wasn't married yet. Myra writes: "About 1926." Probable. Then group pictures without my grandfather. Nechuma looks much older in them.

First row, from right: Moyshe and Nechuma (neé Parnes) Sztajnlauf, parents of Runia, Eric, Wolf, and Shmuel Tsvi (who died as a child); Runia's mother-in-law or Nechuma's sister. Second row, from right: Eric, Runia, Runia's husband Bolek. According to Myra Steinlauf Fischer, c. 1926. Copyright Michael Steinlauf.

Grandmother Nechuma is listed in the Central Database of Shoah Victims at Yad Vashem.

Moyshe Sztajnlauf, second from left. Palestine, mid-1920's. Copyright Michael Steinlauf.

Moyshe Sztajnlauf (1873–1930), Michael Steinlauf's paternal grandfather, on the right. Copyright Michael Steinlauf.

1920s. Same group as previous photo taken some years later. Moyshe Sztajnlauf on the right, holding a copy of the Hebrew newspaper *Haaretz*. Copyright Michael Steinlauf.

Summer at resort. From the right: Wolf, Nechuma, Mietek, Runia, Izio, Bolek. According to Myra Steinlauf-Fischer, c. 1937. Copyright Michael Steinlauf.

From the right: Runia, Nechuma, Wolf. Copyright Michael Steinlauf.

Nechuma. Copyright Michael Steinlauf.

Runia had two sons. The older one was named Izio, the younger one Mietek. You can sense the prosperity. This was the upper middle class, the bourgeoisie. They were all killed.

This is my father with Izio on his shoulder. Behind them a thin pine forest. On the back in pen is the date: 23 August 1930. In Polish.

Wolf Sztajnlauf with Izio, Runia's elder son, August 23, 1930. Copyright Michael Steinlauf.

Runia with younger son, Mietek, September, 1934. Copyright Michael Steinlauf.

Runia, c. 1940, according to Myra Steinlauf-Fischer. On the reverse the stamp FOTO/"MIMOSA"/Warszawa, [number illegible, perhaps 32] Twarda Street. Copyright Michael Steinlauf.

EJ: Runia, 1940. From an identity card.

MS: Very beautiful. Very changed. Almost unrecognizable. In that year in Warsaw the Germans set up and closed off the ghetto.

EJ: And here is Michał Sztajnlauf. Why does Myra write: "This photo was taken a short while before the Gestapo took him away to his death"? Did she know anything about this?

MS: I don't know. [Silence.] The photographs are of an idyllic family. No armbands, hunger, fear. No typhus epidemic. No eating corpses.[10] Prosperity, safety. Good looking, young, well-dressed, well-nourished people. Warsaw ghetto, 1941. Hard to imagine the effort it must have taken, first, to create these photographs, and then to save them. And for everything to look so absolutely effortless. [Silence.] I'd never seen these photographs. I didn't know they existed. When I first saw them, I was shaken.

Here he is reclining in his mother's arms. January 1941. Twelfth of January. He's wearing his little shoes; his feet are otherwise bare. You can see that the room must be well-heated. And here he's sitting up in his crib. May 1941. Second of May. So, he's certainly half a year old, half a year and then some.

EJ: He could be even a year old. His face looks like that of a year-old child. The same with his hair. In the January photograph you can see marks on the soles of his shoes, as if he had tried to walk already or at least to stand holding onto something. Or maybe the shoes had been passed on from another child. In any case, it looks as if in January 1941 he was seven or eight months old. That's how I tried to reconstruct it up until yesterday. That's when I received last minute information. From twenty-six years ago, to be exact. This morning I looked into the database of Yad Vashem. And you won't believe it, but he's there. Maryś Sztajnlauf-Rajbenbach. Name

---

10 There were at least two such cases in the ghetto. Both concerned women who were dying of hunger and ate the corpses of their dead children. See Barbara Engelking and Jan Grabowski, *"Żydów łamiących prawo należy karać śmiercią!". "Przestępczość" Żydów w Warszawie 1939-1942* (Warsaw: Stowarzyszenie Centrum Badań nad Zagładą Żydów, 2010).

Renia (Regina, Rywka) Rajbenbach-Sztajnlauf with son Michał (Maryś, Moyshe), Warsaw Ghetto, January 12, 1941. Copyright Michael Steinlauf.

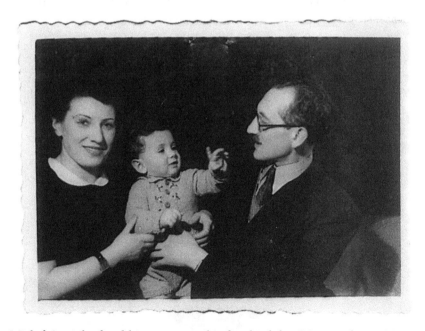

Michał Sztajnlauf and his parents on his first birthday, Warsaw ghetto, May 2, 1941. Copyright Michael Steinlauf.

Michał Sztajnlauf on his first birthday, Warsaw ghetto, May 2, 1941. Copyright Michael Steinlauf.

spelled with Polish diacriticals. Son of Wolf Sztajnlauf and Regina, Renia Rajbenbach, who we know as Rywka. Born in Warsaw, May 2, 1940.[11]

MS: Truly. It's him.

EJ: His death was reported by Stefania Walewska, resident of Tel Aviv at 7 Brodzki Street. Does that tell you anything?

MS: Nothing at all. It sounds like a name from her Aryan papers, which she could of course have kept, but it seems rather as if she'd prefer to give neither her Jewish nor her Israeli identity. In the section "relationship," she calls herself *doda,* meaning aunt.

EJ: Aunt, that is, someone from the mother's family. Perhaps the mother herself.

MS: But the mother knew the date of his death, would certainly have given it.

EJ: The submission was recorded on March 11, 1989. There's also a photograph. The photograph is part of the series taken on May 2, 1941, that is, on the first birthday of Moyshe-Michał-Maryś. That's why his mother is wearing a holiday dress, the father a tie, and he himself rompers embroidered in flowers with toys all around him. These are his birthday presents.

MS: So that on July 22, 1942, when the deportation began, he was two years, two months, and three weeks old. He could certainly walk and would have started talking. See how they look at the child. And the child at them. Light of their eyes. The firstborn. He has everything. I can't look at this. And now we're bringing it into the realm of the visible.

EJ: In one of the German photographs, we see the underside. Warsaw ghetto. May 1941. Young men with armbands have been herded onto a flatbed truck, then crowded together on the platform. Warmly dressed,

---

11 Yad Vashem, Central Database of Shoah victims. http://db.yadvashem.org/names/ nameDetails.html?itemId=1779394&language=en

Prisoners of the ghetto being taken for forced labor on the Aryan side of Warsaw. On the left, with mustache and glasses, Wolf Sztajnlauf. Warsaw, north side of Grzybowska Street; on the right the building of the Judenrat at Grzybowska 24; May 1941. Phot. Ludwig Knobloch, Propagandakompanien der Wehrmacht— Heer und Luftwaffe. Copyright Bundesarchiv Koblenz, Federal Republic of Germany.

with bags hung across their chests. Their hands are mostly in their pockets. Forced laborers. At a certain moment, clearly, they were commanded to look at the camera, because even those who stood with their backs to the camera have looked around. They obey the command. Each in his own way. They know they're being humiliated, in the situation of non-humans. So that, as they look, their entire bearing and the fact that they're looking from above makes us feel as if they're transcending their situation. Their gaze doesn't construct this situation but deconstructs it. The communication they impart is: "We were photographed like antediluvian animals." That's how Jankiel Wiernik, who survived Treblinka, described it.[12] Similar words recur in various Holocaust testimonies.

---

12 Jankiel Wiernik, *Rok w Treblince* (Warsaw: Rada Ochrony Pamięci Walk i Męczeństwa, 2003), p. 13.

MS: My father is standing halfway back on the left. Easy to recognize. The only one with a mustache and glasses.

EJ: The photograph is part of the collections of the Bundesarchiv in Koblenz, which today does business with the trophies of this safari.

MS: Outrageous.

EJ: Enjoyable and useful. Something from nothing. The rights to reproduction cost more than an academic institution such as the Institute of Slavic Studies of the Polish Academy of Sciences, where I work, can afford. But the director, Anna Engelking, read our conversation—back when it only existed as a raw transcription—and decided to purchase the photograph. I mention this because Professor Engelking would like to sincerely thank the Bundesarchiv Koblenz, and there's no other way to do this. There's no place on its website to do it. Originally, I even wrote a request to reduce the cost of the photograph and had it translated into German. Father. Son. Unique trace. Non-profit. Academic purposes. There was even the word Holocaust.

MS: And this could have disturbed someone unnecessarily.

EJ: That's it. I was unable to send it. That's why the Institute of Slavic Studies acquired the photograph by way of purchase. *Merci, l'Allemagne!* Not to mention that if not for the Third Reich we wouldn't have this modest—though pricey—memento.

MS: Jan Jagielski, who was in charge of documenting artifacts at the Jewish Historical Institute, identified where the photograph was taken.[13] The truck is standing on Grzybowska, at number 24, that is, on the northern side of the street, just next to the Judenrat. So, this is what's underneath, inside the lining of the family album.

So here I should talk about that manuscript of my father's that he wrote in Naples just after the war. We don't know what made him decide

---

13 MS adds: Here I would like to pay a brief homage to Jan Jagielski (1937–2021). Janek was one of the very first Poles, half a century ago, to begin to unearth the past of Polish Jews. He devoted the rest of his life to this mission. Honor to his memory.

to write. Nor do we know who he was writing for. Though it doesn't seem that he was writing for himself.

He wrote with a fountain pen on both sides of some yellow lined office paper that was printed in places. It's hard to read by now but fortunately, thanks to Helena Datner,[14] there's a typewritten copy. Strangely there's very little in it about my father himself, about his own experiences. In his thinking it was probably supposed to be a kind of panoramic view, I guess, of the whole ghetto—paradoxically less interesting, at least for me. Also, more prone to factual errors. That was the opinion of Barbara Engelking[15] who I showed it to.

EJ: Your father mentions that he lived at Muranowska 3.[16] He also talks about his little child, but without mentioning its name or gender.

MS: "I return home, broken. I'm greeted by the quizzical, wise look of my year-old child. It stretches its little hands out to me, smiles. [...] That's what Hitler's number one enemy looks like! The 'great and powerful' one fights him, throws into battle the entire mechanism of warfare. My child and similar Jewish children are his opponents. Hysterical laughter rips from my throat, tears choke my larynx. The child's soothing warm little hand interrupts my sad musings. Its sweet babble pushes my sadness away, recalls me to life, pointing to its loveliest moments. It will work out somehow, I think to myself."

This passage makes me think of an account of people as they were herded into the gas chamber at Birkenau, written by a member of the *Sonderkommando*.[17] The writer, who was later killed in an uprising at the

---

14 Sociologist, research scholar at the Jewish Historical Institute [ŻIH] in Warsaw, past president of the Warsaw Jewish Community, and member of the board of directors of the Association of Jewish Communities in Poland.

15 Psychologist, founder and director of the Polish Center for Holocaust Research in Warsaw, part of the Institute of Philosophy and Sociology at the Polish Academy of Sciences.

16 Muranowska was at the northeastern corner of the ghetto, an area mentioned by Jan Karski in Claude Lanzmann's film *Shoah*. During the Jewish uprising it was under the control of the Jewish Military Union created by the Zionist Revisionist youth (Betar). It was the site of the largest battle of the uprising.

17 "Special squad" forced by the Nazis to hurry Jews into the gas chambers, then bury and later unearth and burn their bodies.

camp, buried his text near the crematorium.[18] In both cases I was stricken by the banality of the writing, which conceals more than it reveals, helpless against the horror.

EJ: Scholars of Gradowski's text—his editor Aurélia Kalisky[19] or Noah Benninga—are of a different opinion on this subject, but I understand that such is your feeling. Returning to the passage you cited, this is the only place in which your father writes about himself at any length. About the fact that he was in the Kettle, he writes off-handedly, without a word of commentary. And in the singular. The child could have no longer been alive, but more probably it was with its mother in a hideout, because before the Kettle, the families of the *placówkarze* [those taken out daily to work] weren't touched, so they were still alive. The Kettle was the so-called Great Reduction [*Wielka Redukcja*] carried out during the great liquidation of 1942. A kind of selection within a selection, an *Aktion* within an *Aktion*. It played out in the general area of the Umschlagplatz.[20] There the Germans imprisoned and later deported to Treblinka the majority of the "privileged," who they had previously deluded, telling them that they would remain in the ghetto, that is, stay alive. These "privileged" were forced laborers, doctors and medical personnel, employees of the Judenrat and its institutions, and functionaries of the Jewish *Ordnungsdienst*, as well as their families. In this context your father particularly noted that the families of the *Ordnungsdienst* were shipped out to death, and they themselves, in their overwhelming majority, were shot. He does not, however, mention how he escaped with his life. About those in hiding places—that is, those who despite German orders, did not go to the Kettle—he writes impersonally. Not a word about Nechuma or Runia.

---

18 Zalmen Gradowski, "The Czech Transport: A Chronicle of the Auschwitz *Sonderkommando*," trans. from the Yiddish by Robert Wolf, in David G. Roskies, ed., *The Literature of Destruction: Jewish Responses to Catastrophe* (Philadelphia: The Jewish Publication Society, 1988), pp. 548–69.

19 Salmen Gradowski, *Die Zertrennung: Aufzeichnungen eines Mitglieds des Sonderkommandos*, ed. by Aurélia Kalisky, trans. from Yiddish by Almut Seiffert and Miriam Trinh, introd. and epilogue by Aurélia Kalisky (Berlin: Jüdischer Verlag im Suhrkamp Verlag, 2019).

20 Area in the Warsaw ghetto where Jews were forced onto trains to Treblinka.

MS: Puzzling. He doesn't write about those closest to him, but about the marginal—it would seem—Poles.

EJ: First in the context of their deals smuggling food into the ghetto for big money, then in the context of smuggling Jews out of the ghetto for diamonds and gold. He also mentions the Polish Police, that blockaded the ghetto arm in arm with the Latvians and the SS during the great deportation.

MS: But he doesn't write what he would later repeat, that the most false was the Polish intelligentsia.

EJ: Lying to others, or rather lying to themselves. The intelligentsia needed to look good in its own eyes and this often led Jews to misconceptions whose consequences could be deadly. But there's another piece about the Polish Police—which your father always capitalizes. This time it concerns Jews fleeing the burning ghetto through the sewers during the uprising in 1943: "But most of the sewer exits are guarded on the Aryan side by the Polish Police. The fortunate one who finally made it to an exit had to pay the Polish Police big money for letting him go. Often enough, it would happen that, having taken the money, they would deliver the escapee into the hands of the Gestapo. All those favored by fate who managed to flee the walls of the burning ghetto emerged into a new torturous conspiratorial life among Poles poisoned by the venom of hitlerism."

MS: His mention of the Kettle is the last time he talks about himself in the ghetto. Evidence that he didn't make anything up. I assume that he got out to the Aryan side sometime between the end of the great deportation at the end of September '42 and the first Jewish resistance in January '43. About the latter, he writes only in the third person.[21] He's impressed by

---

21 After the first Jewish armed resistance in January 1943, the Germans withdrew from the ghetto, and returned in April, triggering the ghetto uprising.

the attacks on Szmerling[22] as well as Lejkin[23] and his adjutant Czapliński.[24] He also writes, probably in error, about the attack on Szeryński.[25]

EJ: There was an attack. During the great deportation, even before the Kettle. Szeryński was shot by his subordinate, Izrael Kanał, who was also a member of Akiba,[26] and later of the ŻOB. Szeryński was wounded, but he survived. Sometime later he committed suicide. In your father's text there are no details, and the emotions are muted.

MS: One brief mention though meant a lot to me. In the ghetto, he was apparently offered a job with the Jewish *Ordnungsdienst*. He spoke Polish well and had the right class background. He could have fed his family more easily. He turned it down, sensed the slippery slope that working for the police might have meant. When I read this, I almost forgave him for everything else....

By the way, did you notice where I left those pictures for you?

EJ: You left them in the name of Helena Datner, someone very close to us both, in whose home you've lived and who I meet with frequently.

MS: I left them because I'd lost contact with you.

EJ: Clearly. I understood that you wanted to teach me a lesson. Because you didn't leave them with Helena but at the Museum of the History of Polish Jews. I had to go to the Museum and politely ask. You wanted me to grovel.

---

22 Mieczysław Szmerling—before the war a small businessman; in the ghetto, in the Jewish *Ordnungsdienst*; during the great deportation, assigned by the Germans to serve at the Umschlagplatz. Shot by the Germans in 1943.

23 Jakub Lejkin (1906–42)—a lawyer before the war; in the ghetto, deputy commander of the Jewish *Ordnungsdienst*. Shot by Eliahu Różański of the ŻOB.

24 Stanisław Czapliński—small businessman before the war; in the ghetto, adjutant to Józef Szeryński.

25 Józef Szeryński (1892 or 1893–1943)—Jewish convert to Catholicism; before the war a high officer in the Polish State Police and a member of the authoritarian and antisemitic Camp of National Unity [Obóz Zjednoczenia Narodowego, OZN]; in the ghetto, commander of the Jewish *Ordnungsdienst* under the Polish "blue police".

26 Zionist youth group.

MS: That wasn't it. I left them opposite the monument, where so many things come together.

EJ: I'm curious in what spirit.

MS: Not ironically, that here's a Jew bringing coals to Newcastle. It's far different than irony. You receive the photographs of my brother, of my family, in this place. Here, where they died. And the Museum is a memorial to Jewish life.

EJ: Polin. "Paradisus Judaeorum."[27]

MS: There wasn't any talk of Polin at the beginning, and after "Paradisus Judaeorum" there was supposed to have been a question mark.

EJ: Meanwhile Polin is there, and there's no question mark after *Paradisus Judaeorum.*

MS: Are we supposed to end the world over one non-existent question mark?

EJ: It's about the lens through which the Museum decrees that we have to look. Since "Paradisus Judaeorum" comes out of an antisemitic pamphlet and is an antisemitic trope that still lives in the myth of Judaeopolonia, perhaps it shouldn't be used as a rubric for describing reality. No, I'm beside myself! Will this violence never end?! Must one absolutely necessarily violate corpses and rubble?!

MS: The rubble in the exhibit was supposed to be real, from Muranów, and not papier-maché. Yes, I know. Barbara arranged this. Ask her.[28]

---

27 An early section of the permanent exhibition of the Polin Museum was originally supposed to have had the title "Paradisus Judaeorum?", that is, with a question mark.

28 Barbara Kirshenblatt-Gimblett, curator of the permanent exhibition.

EJ: I don't have to. "We have to overcome the power of the ground …"[29] Among all the experts only Helena Datner—who was in charge of the postwar and post-1989 galleries—had the courage to denounce the implementation of the antisemitic narrative and to resign from the MHŻP. She was also the only one to reveal and oppose Polish state censorship.[30]

I see what's going on, but I'm unable to understand it. It's not only about Warsaw. How to explain, for example, the words of Janusz Makuch, the director of the Jewish Culture Festival in Kraków, that he proclaimed this year at the final concert "Shalom on Szeroka Street"? You heard this with your own ears: "No more antisemitism! No more antipolonism! No more antinazism! Good, positive feelings only!" This happened the day before yesterday, July 4, on the anniversary of the Kielce pogrom to boot.

MS: This works ideally for you, so I'll respond in my characteristic way: I forgive him. He said it at two in the morning after a seven-hour concert.

EJ: Except does it help us in understanding the processes occurring before our eyes and in which we participate—as protest, as affirmation, as looking from the sides? Meanwhile, the documents and photographs that you brought now remain in the closet in my hallway. It makes me feel like a genuine Pole.

---

29 This sentence, often repeated by Kirshenblatt-Gimblett, was used in soliciting submissions to the architectural competition for the building of the museum. See Konrad Matyjaszek, "Wall and Window: The Rubble of the Warsaw Ghetto as the Narrative Space of the Museum of the History of Polish Jews," *Studia Litteraria et Historica* nr. 5 (2016), pp. 1–33. See also Elżbieta Janicka, "The Embassy of Poland in Poland: The Polin Myth in the Museum of the History of Polish Jews," *Studia Litteraria et Historica* nr. 5 (2016), pp. 1–76. Both texts reprinted in *Poland and Polin: New Interpretations in Polish-Jewish Studies*, ed. by Irena Grudzińska-Gross and Iwa Nawrocki (Frankfurt am Main: Peter Lang Verlag, 2016), pp. 59–98 and 121–171, respectively.

30 "Jankiel, chasydzi i Tuwim. O Muzeum Historii Żydów Polskich z Heleną Datner rozmawia Piotr Paziński," *Midrasz*, 2015 (1), pp. 5–10; "Z Heleną Datner rozmawia Poldek Sobel," *Plotkies*, 2014 (62); "Datner: Żydowski punkt widzenia. Pyta Kacha Szaniawska," *Dziennik Opinii Krytyka Polityczna*, May 30, 2015: https://krytykapolityczna.pl/kultura/historia/datner-zydowski-punkt-widzenia-rozmowa/.

Family vacation of the Sacks and Steinlaufs. Zev (son) kneeling, behind him Deborah Sack (partner) and Michael, next to them Ben (son) with Gabriel (son) on his shoulders. Jamaica, November 29, 2014. Copyright Deborah Sack and Michael Steinlauf.

MS: I'll reclaim them in September, when I'll be here to give a talk on the hundredth anniversary of Peretz's death. I'd like to spend some more time in Poland. A lot of interesting and important things are happening. But I lack having other than white people around. And I'd like to have my family with me because I miss them. Zev and Ben have their own lives now.

EJ: But Deborah and Gabriel will doubtless be delighted.

MS: You can be ironic if you want, but Deborah really likes it here. The problem is that Gabriel needs to be raised in a culture and society that's created at least partly by people like him. Black.

Chapter 10

Postscripts

Michael Steinlauf, Fall 2021

In October 2015, three months after the final conversation recorded above, my own narrative as well as Poland's were profoundly disrupted. For Poland, this meant the consecutive parliamentary and presidential victories of the Law and Justice Party (Prawo i Sprawiedliwość, PiS). For the past six years, Poland has been governed by a right-wing nationalist, so-called populist, political party whose roots lie in the proto-fascist Endecja of the interwar years. PiS has transformed political discourse in general, and discourse about "Jewish matters" in particular. Poland, according to their narrative, is once more the nation of heroes and martyrs. One year later, a political eruption in the United States, comparable in many ways to the Polish one: Donald Trump was elected president. According to Trump and his Red Hats, America would be great once again. Meanwhile, also in October 2015, I was brought low by a stroke which led to weeks of rehabilitation before I was able to resume some of my previous life. I continued to seek closure in the narrative of my brother, and I believe I finally attained it in July 2018 at the Borderlands Foundation in Sejny, Poland. There I collaborated with Raphael Rogiński, Michael Alpert, Krzysztof Czyżewski and the Sejny Klezmer Orchestra to stage a production entitled "Misterium of the Dark Brother;" https://www.youtube.com/watch?v=axLDIv74blA. My dybbuk was permitted the *tikkun* [redemptive transformation] of entering the realm of art. This seems proper closure for the narrative of my brother. The renewed worldwide struggle for democracy and humanity, however, has only begun. It is my hope that the present exchange may contribute a bit in its own way to this struggle.

Elżbieta Janicka, Fall 2021

From the perspective of someone who lives on the ground in Poland and has to endure the consequences of this fact, the second rise to power of the Law and Justice Party in 2015 (the first was in 2005–07) and the consequent collapse of liberal democracy cannot be understood as a simple disruption. The reality we live in Poland today was ideologically prepared by the long rule of the neoliberal Civic Platform (2007–15) which—instead of opposing—legitimized, deepened and strengthened the national radical historical politics of the first Law and Justice government. In today's Poland, the lie that Poles were not the perpetrators of the Jedwabne massacre has become state doctrine; the Polish prime minister has paid tribute to Polish Nazi collaborators; the murderers of Jews are being rehabilitated, praised, and celebrated; antisemitic lies and hatred are taught in public schools; and Polish neo-fascist organizations are financed by the state. Today's Poland is an "elective dictatorship" that envisions to quit the European Union—membership in which was the country's main historical achievement. None of this has impelled the architects of the pre-2015 symbolic order—among them the creators of the Museum of the History of Polish Jews and Polish activists of the so-called revival of Jewish life—to question their share of responsibility for the current state of affairs. This responsibility is epitomized in the main principle they chose to follow, namely, careful avoidance of all confrontation with the dominant Polish culture and satisfaction of the expectations of the Polish majority. As a result, the authors' opinions diverge more today than in 2014 when these conversations began.

Index

"A memoir in the guise of an intense, sometimes furious discussion, *This Was Not America* opens a window on Polish-Jewish history and peers at it through the eyes of an American-Jewish historian and a Polish anthropologist engaged in an animated give-and-take. Their conversation plunges readers into the depths of Polish-Jewish relations, bringing dozens of forgotten figures and their work to life as Steinlauf and Janicka weave their ways through their own personal stories and their connections to a highly contentious Polish-Jewish past. Raw and evocative, their discussion gives nuance and detail to Polish-Jewish history and Polish-Jewish relations of the late 20th century where the personal is political and vice-versa."

—Eddy Portnoy, author of
Bad Rabbi and Other Strange but
True Stories from the Yiddish Press

"This book is one of a kind, a must read for anyone interested in Polish Jewish relations and the impact of the Holocaust on the second generation. It is honest, absorbing and thought-provoking."

—Samuel D. Kassow,
Charles H. Northam
Professor of History, Trinity College

"This brutally honest dialogue soars above the institutions, power structures, and discourses that have too often served to tame an unsettling Polish/Jewish past. Eschewing the kinds of compromises that inevitably favor the dominant culture, Janicka and Steinlauf produce a truth-wound that is the beginning of genuine healing."

—Glenn Dynner, author of *Yankel's Tavern:*
Jews, Liquor, & Life in the Kingdom of Poland

"A required reading for anyone who wonders how an antisemitic authoritarianism is possible today in the former land of Eastern European Jewry. The first book to raise the question of American Jewish share of responsibility for this state of affairs."

—Helena Datner,
scholar of Jewish social history
and antisemitism in Poland

CPSIA information can be obtained
at www.ICGtesting.com
Printed in the USA
BVHW011356231022
649933BV00002B/2